SEDO...
BEYOND THE VORTEX

An Ascension Manual
And Remembrance of the Sacred Science Of The Soul

Creating The New Age Of Planetary Peace
And Healing Through The Use Of Collective Consciousness

By RICHARD DANNELLEY

Beyond the Vortex is an important statement about the relation between Soul Awareness, Vortex Phenomenon, Sacred Geometry, the Merkaba, the Medicine Wheel, and Ascension. By using the meditations and practices that are detailed in this book, we can learn to use "Vortex Energy," to activate our crystalline Body of Light (the Merkaba). Anyone who is interested in the possibility of Ascension will find this book to be of great interest.

Also by Richard Dannelley:
Sedona Power Spot, Vortex, and Medicine Wheel Guide
Sedona UFO Connection

SEDONA:
BEYOND THE VORTEX

The Ultimate Journey to Your Personal Place of Power

Second Edition, Revised October 1995

– SOUL STAR OF SEDONA –

ISBN 0-9629453-7-4

PUBLISHED BY THE VORTEX SOCIETY
P.O. Box 948, Sedona, Arizona 86339
520-634-6703

Book design and graphics by Richard Dannelley
Cover mandala with Kokopelli and Babalu by Richard Dannelley

Computer graphics by David Work
Typeset by Michael Tyree

Printed in Sedona, Arizona, by Light Technology

DISCLAIMER

The author, the publisher, the Vortex Society and Soul Star of Sedona accept no responsibility for damages that might be incurred as a result of engaging in any of the physical, ceremonial, or spiritual exercises detailed in this manual or taught in the Soul Star of Sedona course. People suffering from mental disorders, epilepsy or fundamentalism are advised to refrain from engaging in any of the aforementioned exercises and practices.

PRIVATE SESSIONS – LECTURES – CLASSES – CEREMONIES

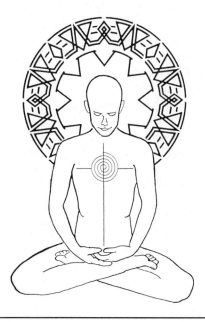

Since the release of my first book in 1991 (*Sedona Power Spot, Vortex, and Medicine Wheel Guide*) I have had the opportunity to learn many amazing things, and I am now ready to pass my knowledge on to individual students and to groups.

I have gained the ability to teach most people how to access the energies I describe in this book in one lesson, and I am available for private sessions.

I am also available as a guest speaker, or ceremonial leader for tour groups in Sedona. And I am actively seeking people who would like to sponsor my lectures and seminars throughout the country.

If you are interested in working with me, or you would like to receive a special Vortex Society newsletter please send a self-addressed-stamped-envelope to:

The Vortex Society – Soul Star
P.O. Box 948
Sedona, Arizona 86339

I also want to mention that I try to read all of my mail, and I am interested in hearing what you have to say. As you may be able to imagine, however, I found that I do not have the time to answer all of my mail, so be sure to include a self-addressed stamped-envelope along with your letters so I can send you something.

Richard Dannelley

TABLE OF CONTENTS

THE WORK OF PATRICK AND GAEL FLANAGAN

Sri Yantra pictograph by Bill Witherspoon
Photograph courtesy James Deardorff and UFO Magazine.

Sedona, Arizona, has gained a well-deserved reputation as a place of mysterious power. I have been exploring these powers for several years, and I am now ready to share the results of my research into the Vortex Phenomenon and related subjects. I was born about 48 miles from Sedona in Prescott, Arizona, and I am the author of the *Sedona Power Spot, Vortex, and Medicine Wheel Guide*, which is considered by many to be the definitive statement about the Sedona Vortex Phenomena and the use of Non-traditional Medicine Wheel ceremonies for healing the Earth.

I have found that the Vortices have a direct relation to the primal forces of creation and that many important things can be learned by studying Vortex phenomenon. A few of the things that are worthy of noting in this introduction are:

By "tuning in" to Vortex energy we can improve and probably extend our lives, as Vortex energy is one of the things that create life. An excellent example of this is genetic material or "DNA:" the twin spirals of DNA create a Vortex as they rotate through time.

Rotation is one of the primal forces in the Universe: all things are spiraling through time. As human beings we can easily gain access to the power of Universal Vortex energy by using what is known as the Merkaba meditation to make our personal energy fields rotate. As we gain the power to rotate our personal energy fields at high speeds we gain access to some very interesting powers.

The creation of the Merkaba (the perfected Light Body) is the goal of human evolution. With the Merkaba we can direct immense amounts of healing energy into the Earth. Many of you who read these words understand what I am talking about. Even if you have not had much experience in working with these energies or studying these things. This is because it is natural for you to intuitively know how to work with these energies, and the desire for you to do so exists. All you need to remember – *to remember* – is contained in this book.

The forces that I describe in this book are not limited to Sedona, and it is not necessary for you to come here in order to benefit from them. In fact, one of the most important things that will be accomplished by this book is that many people in all parts of the world will read these words and learn that they can create energy Vortices, Merkabas, and Group Merkaba/Medicine Wheels in the place where they live, and that by doing so we can heal our planet.

In this lifetime, my original inspiration to look beyond the veil of mundane reality was found in the books of Carlos Castaneda, who wrote about his experiences with a Native American mystic who worked with "power spots" and traveled between dimensions. Over the years since then, I have practiced various forms of yoga and applied metaphysics, and as I have matured, my ability to work with spiritual energy has also increased. Yet, like most people, when I first started practicing working with these energies I saw very little "light" when I closed my eyes and felt almost nothing. Now, after playing at it for several years I have learned to do some pretty exotic things with spiritual energy, and I have learned how to pass my knowledge on to others.

One of the most important realizations I have had in this work is that *whatever we see within our mind's eye exists*, even if it is nothing more than an energy pattern in the mind, and that the more energy we give our thoughts, the more manifest they become. With this realization I found I could go beyond disbelief and truly begin acting as an energy channel in the creation of energy fields and Vortices.

Projecting energy and creating energy fields is easier than you might think. Where thought goes, energy flows. We can create any type of energy field or vibrational color just by seeing it with our mind's eye. One of the most important things to remember in the study of the mastery of Light is that the more we practice, the more real our work becomes. When I first started in this work I did not see or feel energy, or so I thought. Nonetheless, I kept practicing until I did. It was just as my teachers said: **"Do the exercises and things will happen, whether you see the energy or not."**

I find it quite interesting that so many people have become interested in the Medicine Wheel and Native American teachings in the past few years. I see this as a result of two things: first, many Americans of European descent have strong past-life connections to Native American culture; secondly, we know intuitively that ceremonies that are similar to the Medicine Wheel open up the interdimensional portals that allow the Christ Consciousness energies to enter the planetary grid.

As for the concept of Americans of European descent having past lives as Native Americans, this seems to be in harmony with the law of karma and the prophecies of various Native American seers from the 1800s to our current days. Thus, it is plain to see that at this time in our history a large part of our national karma has to do with reconciling the beauty and the pain of the native peoples. It is therefore very healthy for those of us who are of European descent to participate in ceremonies such as the traditional Medicine Wheel, the sweat lodge, and the pipe, etc., but we must avoid getting trapped in the past and remember to keep moving forward into *new interpretations of that which is so ancient.*

Most Americans of European descent who study Native American teachings follow the Medicine Wheel teachings of the Plains tribes that are similar to those which were taught by Sun Bear. These teachings are beautiful and powerful, but it must be understood that for the most part they reflect their originating tribe's interpretations of the universe, which in many ways were valid only for those people in the days when they lived. This is why I neither follow nor attempt to teach the old traditions. Those days are gone.

We are fortunate, however, that the native people of this land anchored the energy of these ceremonies into the Earth, and that their lineage preserved the essence of the teachings for us to rediscover. If it were not for this we would surely be lost.

The concept of the Medicine Wheel is a teaching that is given to all humans so that they can reaffirm their connection to the Source of All Things as they walk their evolutionary path. In the final phase of ascension the Medicine Wheel becomes the Merkaba of ascension, the jeweled vehicle of redemption from the lower worlds. In this, its highest form, the Medicine Wheel ceremony is the application of Vortex technology.

In closing this part of the discussion I want to go on record and say that I apparently have a very strong connection to past lives as a Native American shaman. I do not, however, dwell on this or make any attempt to become an Indian in this life. My knowledge and my teaching in this life are empowered by events of the past and tempered by the full knowledge that we must go forward, creating a reality that is based in the present, with our vision looking to the future.

So I ask you to study this book with an open mind, allowing yourself to find new interpretations of that which is so ancient. Avoid allowing yourself to get stuck in old patterns that might limit you or hold you back.

Perhaps you will be inspired to study this subject and become a professional ascension facilitator. Each community must produce people who are qualified to take other people through these processes. In other words, some of you are being prepared to do more than simply transform yourselves; you are also being prepared to help others transform themselves. Not everyone can come to Sedona to study. Some of you who read these words must take it upon yourselves to research the art of working with spiritual Light for healing and mental clearing in order to ultimately become transformation counselors for the people of your local community.

All things are the gift of the Great Spirit,
and the Great Spirit is abundant in its gifts.

UNDERSTANDING THE VORTEX

In this book we will not be going deeply into the exploration of the Vortex phenomena in Sedona, instead we will be exploring the Vortex as a universal quality that is present in all things. The meditations and ceremonies in this book can be used at any of the Vortices, but even more importantly, they can be used to help you access the ascension energies and build your Diamond Body of Light, or Merkaba, as you go about your life in the place where you live.

Interest in the Vortex phenomena in Sedona goes back quite a bit further than many people realize. Last year, in 1994, I met a man who was traveling here from France who told me that the famous Dada artist, Max Ernst, had published a book in French that relates his experiences with Vortices and crystal cities below Sedona during the time he lived here in the 1930's! As for historical evidence that I can validate which establishes a date for the discovery of the Vortices in Sedona, 1963 is the year the founders of the Rainbow Ray Focus established their center next to the Airport Vortex. This refutes the popular belief that the channel Page Bryant "discovered" the Vortices in Sedona. In fact, I myself knew of the Vortices perhaps as many as four years before she arrived here.

As for what the Vortices in Sedona are, this is a subject that is open to debate. Some of the more uptight and reactionary members of the community say that they are either a complete fantasy or a fabrication perpetrated long ago by a fringe element in the local Chamber of Commerce. As for myself, I can say that while I am not entirely sure what the Vortices are, I am still certain that they exist: I can feel their power and see the effect they have on both believers and nonbelievers. Yet I cannot say with certainty exactly what the Vortices are.

As I said in my first book, *Sedona Power Spot, Vortex, and Medicine Wheel Guide*, there are certain geological characteristics found in this area, such as faults and deposits of magnetized basalt, that probably do have something to do with the formation of Vortices. Since then I have also determined that the Vortices of Sedona have a relation to variations in the Earth's gravity field due to the transition between mountains and flatlands. But after studying the Vortices for several years, I have found that there are aspects of this phenomena that go far beyond mundane geological explanations.

Various channels have said the Vortices are "electromagnetic." This does not say much, however, as everything in the known universe is electromagnetic. To find an explanation for the Vortices in Sedona I have had to expand my awareness and become aware of the fact that universal consciousness has well-defined energy patterns that provide the structure for all things. And that the Vortices should not be explained as being merely an electromagnetic phenomenon, but rather as a nexus in the gridwork of the universe that can provide the human race an entry point into the greater mysteries of human evolution in the ever-expanding life systems of the universe. It is from this standpoint that I now base my research and my teaching.

In physical Earth-plane terms we can see that the Vortices of Sedona have a relationship to the Earth and the universe as a whole that is dependent on our planet's geometrical relation to various stars, constellations, and the other planets of our solar system. As the Earth moves though space these relations change. This in turn creates the ebb and flow of all types of cosmic energies that influence life on our planet. This is why the energy of the Vortices in Sedona and other places may vary considerably from time to time.

As for the theory that there could be crystals within the Earth that cause the Vortex phenomena in Sedona, there could be something to this theory, as there is geological evidence to support the presence of conditions that form quartz crystals, as well as rubies, emeralds, sapphires, and other types of gemstones. One of my theories is that there are large deposits of crystals in fissures that exist deep in the rocks. And that Oak Creek Canyon and Boynton Canyon have notable veins of crystals below them that act as antennas for energies that contribute to the Vortex phenomena.

The energy patternings of sacred geometry that we will study in this book are important basic aspects of the Universal Vortex Phenomenon. Each Vortex, whether permanent or temporary, contains a programming point, or "eye" (or seed) which attaches it, via an energy/consciousness threshold to the singular immovable point in the universe: The Throne of God – The Great Central Sun. The symbol of the eye, as it is used in religious and metaphysical imagery has a direct relationship to this programming point that exists within each Vortex. (See Vesica Piscis in the Sacred Geometry section.)

Vortices are universal; they range in size from subatomic to macrocosmic. The larger a Vortex is, the greater the effect it will have on its surroundings. This effect represents the programming of space with the sacred energies of God. The reason why we are drawn to Vortices, or why we would want to reprogram our aura to become a Vortex/Merkaba, is therefore self-evident: it is because we want to come closer to that which we call God.

Chaos is a state of being in which space is relatively free of Macro-Vortex energy patterning. Christ Consciousness is a state of being in which a locality in the universe is in a state of alignment with the primary energy patternings that emanate from the Throne. When we practice individual Merkaba meditations and do Group Merkaba/Medicine Wheel ceremonies we become more like the perfect energy that emanates from God.

According to *The Keys of Enoch* and countless other sources, the primary energy/substance and consciousness/program of the universe is Love (Universal Life-Force Energy). Love manifests in our electromagnetic universe as the Holy Spirit. Christ Consciousness for human beings is wholly dependent on accessing the energies of Universal Love. The symbol at the bottom of this page is one of the primary symbols of Christ Consciousness.

Which is more powerful: the Bomb, or 144,000 people praying for peace? The answer is, of course, whichever happens first.

In 1984 I was living in the mountains near Los Angeles, California. One day I received a piece of mail that quite literally gave me goose bumps when I took it out of my mailbox. It was an invitation to a Medicine Wheel ceremony that was to be given by a man named Sun Bear.

At that time I was not sure what kind of event this was supposed to be. All I knew was that the power surrounding this invitation was unmistakable. I felt compelled to attend and, as fate had it, it was easy for me to make arrangements to do so because the ceremony was to take place quite near my home. Paying the fee for this event was also easy because I had recently found a few pieces of gold.

At the Medicine Wheel ceremony, I received the vision that guides my life and I saw the truth of Sun Bear's teaching: with ceremony we could heal the Earth and ourselves.

As stated earlier, I had very little idea what a Medicine Wheel ceremony was. All I knew was that the idea of attending the ceremony felt good, and I was ready for whatever was going to happen up there on that mountain. Looking back on this experience I can see that although it was not apparent at the time, I experienced a profound initiation.

Upon arriving at the YMCA camp where the event was to take place I met a man who called himself Bruce Blue Cloud. Bruce was attempting to carry several fairly large rocks to the ceremony and I offered to help, so he gave me two of them and said, "They're special." By the time we arrived at the Wheel, quite a few people were already gathered around it, including several Native Americans dressed in skins and beads. When we reached the edge of the Wheel, we paused for only a brief moment as someone told me to "have respect." Then, with everyone watching, we proceeded to the center of the Wheel where we gave our rocks to the Medicine People waiting there.

After I exited the Wheel, some people on the side showed me how to make tobacco ties (little pieces of cloth with tobacco tied inside with string). "Put your prayers in here," they said. I prayed that I would receive the gift of communication so that I could help people understand what needed to be done to save the Earth. (This is exactly what I am doing now. It gives me shivers down my back to realize this; there is a reason I am writing these words and there is a reason you are reading them. This is the power of the Great Spirit at work.)

I had very little idea what was going on while I was doing these things. It was like going to camp. Yet I can definitely see that there was a great deal of power in our ceremony, and our prayers are still at work changing our world.

After the ceremony we had our choice of several workshops that were going on at different times around the camp. I chose to see Sun Bear himself and arrived early at the clearing where he was to talk. When Sun Bear arrived, he came and sat down right in front of me; however, for the rest of his presentation he pretty much ignored me except to say to me, "You will survive."

A few weeks after the Medicine Wheel ceremony with Sun Bear, I attended a Rainbow World Peace and Healing Gathering. The main focus for these gatherings is the planetary healing ceremony on the Fourth of July. The Rainbow Gatherings are held on Forest Service land in a different state each year. These gatherings are organized by a group of people who attended the first Love-in's in San Francisco. The Love-in's gave way to the "Gathering of the Tribes." (You may have seen the classic '60's poster, Gathering of the Tribes.) A group of powerful people who attended these events received a vision of planetary ascension similar to that recounted in the classic of Native American literature, *Black Elk Speaks*. This vision was of people from all tribes coming together in "the sacred hoop of the nations" (the Medicine Wheel) and ascending to heaven on rainbows of light.

In 1984 the Rainbow Gathering was to be held at Medicine Lake, in the Modoc National Forest in California. This site was about one hundred miles east of Mt. Shasta and also fairly close to San Francisco and Humboldt County. When I arrived at the encampment, I soon heard the rumor circulating around the camp that the Modoc Indians were not happy about the gathering being held at Medicine Lake because this was the place of their tribe's ancestral burial ground. They warned the Rainbow people not to go past the ice on the ridge of the mountain to the west of the encampment, as that was the location of their ancient burial ground. The Modocs also let it be known that the Medicine Lake area was the place where members of their tribe went for their vision quests and that this was the dwelling place of spirits who were known to test people. Everyone in the camp knew they were going to experience Heavy Medicine. Little did I realize that I was being prepared to have a serious shamanic experience that would take me through the veil of death and then return me to the world of the living as a forever-changed man.

The main world peace and healing ceremony of the Rainbow Gatherings occurs on July Fourth. This year the ceremony was to take place in a large alpine meadow. Word had been passed around the camp that the vigil in the meadow would begin before dawn, and that everyone who wanted to take part in the main ceremony should make their way in silence to the meadow at 10 a.m. The silence was to be held until noon, at which time we were to say many unending OMs as we focused our thoughts on world peace and healing. I have included a picture of this ceremony so that you can have a better idea of what it was like. It was incredibly powerful, and I believe that most of the approximately 3000 people who were in that circle were convinced that the power of our prayers had changed planetary destiny. It seems that there was telepathic intercommunication in the meadow. Everyone came together in harmony, and when it was done, the image of the bombs resting safely in their silos was strong in many minds. This ceremony was one of the most wonderful experiences of my life, and everyone was blessed by Spirit. The sacredness of what we were doing was unmistakable. We knew we were changing the course of history. It was *powerful.*

I was one of the few people who took pictures of this event. Most people understood the seriousness of the ceremony and did not allow themselves to become distracted by their cameras. I, however, had received a message from Spirit that I was to record this event and somehow get this story out to the world. Little did I realize that a few years later I was going to write this book.

7

I left the circle feeling rather elated, but upon arriving at my camp a strange feeling of foreboding came over me after one of the people passing by my camp reminded me of what the Modoc Indians had said. As it had turned out, without realizing it I had inadvertently camped just a little way below the burial ground and the ice.

After my visitor left I began to feel even stranger. Suddenly an Indian appeared at my camp, he looked down at some feathers I had laid out for trade and then said to me, "You're crazy. You better put those things away. You do not know what you are messing with: these are the feathers of the night bird of death." Needless to say, this upset me, and soon after he left I put the feathers away.

As I sat there I gradually became aware of the energies of the mountain spirits and began feeling the presence of a consciousness. As I gazed across the valley at Medicine Mountain, a voice spoke to me out of the ethers, saying, "Prepare yourself; you have an appointment." At that point I began to become upset and a little paranoid, so I decided to see if I could walk it off. After gathering up the feathers and my daypack, I started up the mountain trail toward the ice. (I did not intend to cross the ice.) After going up the trail a little way, I felt compelled to stop and gaze at Medicine Mountain. As I stood there I became aware of the chirping of crickets, and as I listened closer, the chirping turned into words: "You shall meet your fate today; prepare to meet your death."

I went into an immediate panic and began running up the mountain. I was going to die! I suddenly found myself lost in a Medicine vision. I ran up the trail in a panic, but due to the altitude, I soon had to stop to catch my breath. As I stood there panting, the crickets began singing to me, "Don't go up that way; the graves are up there. If you cross the ice at the top of the ridge, the spirits will steal your soul. You can get to the top of the mountain through the trees, without crossing the ice. You must make it to the top of the mountain before sundown!"

At that point I can truly say that I absolutely lost it. I began running again but soon found myself out of breath, and so once again I began walking. After a few minutes, I began to calm down, yet, as if being drawn by a magnet, I continued walking upward through the trees, traversing along the side of the mountain, gaining altitude, but not knowing where I was headed.

Suddenly, in the midst of the trees I met a man who seemed familiar to me. I was truly enchanted by his presence and soon forgot about my appointment at the top of the mountain. After we talked for awhile, he invited me down to his camp to meet his friends. Their camp was just below where we were standing, and we were able to make it down there in a matter of minutes. When I walked into the camp I immediately noticed a book lying on a tree stump in the middle of the camp. It was *Rainbow Bridge*. I opened the book and was completely captivated by it. I had, as they say, a high level of resonance with the information about personal and planetary ascension that the *Rainbow Bridge* contains. As I look back on that moment, I can see that Spirit had planned all these things in advance. I was being led through an initiation and being shown my life's work.

One of the things that was odd about this chance meeting was that I felt as if I had known some of the people in the camp before meeting them there on that day. It was very strange. Some of the people, by their appearance, could have been in my immediate family. It seemed as though we were one in spirit.

After a while a man walked into camp who seemed to me to be rather sinister. He looked different from the others in the camp. He was dark and wore a grisly looking Grateful Dead T-shirt. He came right over to where I was standing and started talking to me in a manner that disturbed me. I did not like his energy. At that point I remembered my appointment at the top of the mountain. The Sun would set soon and I wanted to see it happen. I tried to excuse myself from the camp, but this strange man insisted that I stay. This bothered me and I attempted to leave, but then he moved in front of me and stood in my way, blocking my path. The energy of the camp became tense and I suddenly had the feeling that I had to get away from this man, that I *must* see the sunset. Apparently he picked up on my discomfort because his presence became challenging. Suddenly I once again went into a panic, and as the adrenaline rushed into my blood, I pushed him out of my way in a violent manner and began running toward the summit of the mountain.

As I made my way toward the summit, I stopped several times to catch my breath. Each time I stopped I found myself moving farther and farther away from normal reality. The sound of the huge Fourth of July celebration below was maddening! It was an audio landscape out of our primal past. A pagan celebration, wild beyond belief, with drums, singing, and rebel yells moving from one end of the camp to the other, in full stereo. The crescendos of sound drove me into an ever-increasing frenzy. The drums from below seemed to have the power of the heartbeats of every man, woman, and child on the planet. Every time the wild calls and drumming reached a climax, a wave of intense energy raced through my mind. I was being sent into a full shamanic experience that only the Spirit of the Earth could control.

I died when I finally made it to the power spot at the top of the mountain. It was terribly frightening, right down to the moment I gave up and realized I was dead! AHHHH!!!

The death initiation is perhaps the most powerful initiation that a mystic/shaman/yogi must pass through in order to obtain the transcendental vision of reality that is required for mastery. A shaman sees beyond death. Life as a dead man is quite different from *normal* reality. You understand the multidimensional nature of reality; you have no fear. You have seen death and you know that consciousness does not end.

A few moments after I "died" I felt much better. I had transcended fear and limitation. I walked across the broad mountaintop and found a rock I could stand on so I could give myself back to the light of the Sun. As I stood upon the rock waiting to disappear from the face of the Earth, I thought for a moment about God. Then I remembered Robert Anton Wilson's book, *Cosmic Trigger*, and the Sirian connection with extraterrestrial intelligence. I thought, "What if?"

I sent out a cosmic call with my mind: "Are you there, space beings, masters from beyond? I am dead! Are you there?" A vision of an open hand appeared to me. It was made of golden-white light. The palm was facing me and the fingers were pointing upward. I then received a telepathic communication: "We want you to be able to move yourself through space with thought. When you can do this, you will be ready to meet us. You need to learn to become pure energy; you need to learn to dematerialize your body."

I asked, "How do I do this?" The voice replied, "You must concentrate on a spot a few feet from you and use your *Will* to project yourself into that space as you think of yourself as pure energy." I followed the instructions the voice gave me as the voice encouraged my efforts. "Concentrate – good – you are doing well. See how it feels. Now turn your attention to the Sun." (The sun was just setting.) "See the golden light of the Sun? That is your nourishment; become one with the light of the Sun."

As I stared at the huge golden disk on the horizon I thought of Don Juan and the *Tales of Power*. Hadn't Don Juan told Carlos that he should drink in the light of the Sun by gazing indirectly at the setting Sun? I gazed at the Sun and aligned myself with the light. I drank deeply of the Sun's golden nectar. Later that night the stars were very intense.

Two years later, in 1988, I was back in Arizona, living in Sedona. Soon I began attending Medicine Wheel ceremonies that my friends Eagle Feather and John Armbruster were leading at a place known as the Schnebly Hill Medicine Wheel.

This Medicine Wheel was put in place shortly before the Harmonic Convergence in 1987 and has been the focal point for planetary healing ceremonies in Sedona ever since. It is truly a magical place that is obviously cared for by the Great Spirit. The moment I entered the Wheel for the first time, the thunder spoke. I felt the reality of the magic of Sedona and knew I had been welcomed home.

PLANETARY HEALING CEREMONIES

Which is more powerful: the Bomb, or a planetary peace ceremony at just the right time? Those who say that the Harmonic Convergence means nothing, those who say it proves nothing, those who blindly point out the fact that our planet is still in bad shape are the people who are missing the point. The only thing that could happen fast is nuclear annihilation. World peace is a long process of undoing years of disharmonious living.

The original Harmonic Convergence, August 16-17 1987 was the first planetary event of its kind in recorded history. An untold number of people on all parts of the planet came together in ceremony and prayed for world peace and healing. Those of us who hold the vision believe that our ceremonies are largely responsible for the stabilization of the Cold War and the current trend of the disarming of nuclear weapons. We must continually remind ourselves that every moment creates energy that either continues the process of peace or draws us back into darkness, and that every day is a good day for prayer.

It is evident that the Harmonic Convergence was a critical window of opportunity in the space-time matrix of the universe, a time when our species and the soul of the planet itself were to choose to initiate the ascension program or abort. It was a time that required planetary group-consciousness to create the energy wave that would steer our planet away from disaster. It was a total success; we passed the first test.

It is worthy of noting that 1987 was a very dangerous year in the history of our planet. In true harmony with the Mayan Calendar teachings, the days before the Harmonic Convergence found themselves to be a time of great peril in our planetary experiment. In 1986 the American fleet had gone to the Persian Gulf, and as you may remember, things were very tense. In 1986 the United States deployed the Trident III first-strike system to augment the MX missile system. These weapons systems could have been used if we had not "converged."

A BRAVE NEW WORLD

The Iran-Contra hearings were occurring during the time of the Harmonic Convergence. The treasonous plot of the secret government was being exposed (sort of) and, as fate had it, Oliver North's time to testify went right through Harmonic Convergence weekend. (Another strange "coincidence?")

HARMONIC CONVERGENCE II

The second Harmonic Convergence on July 26, 1992, passed without most people hearing a thing about it. In Sedona, however, we made plans for this event months in advance, and several hundred people came into town for the occasion (which was free of charge). This event was well-attended in spite of the fact that most mainstream and New Age publications did not think the event was worthy of their ink.

I was the primary organizer and master of ceremonies of the Harmonic Convergence II event in Sedona. This was one of the most notable events of my life. The energies that ran through me during the ceremonies transformed me and took me to a higher level of awareness. These ceremonies were truly shamanic experiences, both for myself and for the people who shared them with me. The climax of the event occurred during the Sunset ceremony on Sunday, July 26, 1992. As I read the invocation I felt the power of the Great Spirit.

Before the ceremony I arranged an altar centered around a disk which carries the symbol of the Vortex Society (the mandala on the cover of this book). I placed a single rock in the center of the mandala as a symbol of the Earth. Around this piece of basalt and upon the mandala I made a crystal layout, which included some of my personal crystals and some crystals that belonged to various people who were attending the ceremony. (The two invocations that were read each day appear elsewhere in this book.)

After we read the invocations, an inner voice suggested that I use the stone in the center of the circle as a focal point for sending our prayers into the Earth. I walked to the center of the circle of people and put my forehead to the stone. As I did this I told myself that I was to project my consciousness into the Earth and

11

deliver the prayers of the people. The experience was astounding! I sensed my consciousness entering the Earth, and I remember encountering structures of pure energy. After I sensed that I was in contact with the heart/mind of our planet, I announced myself and delivered our prayers for peace and stability and for the awakening of the Christ energies. And as there had been serious earthquakes in California just a few days before this ceremony, I also asked that the Earth below California would remain stable.

By the end of the ceremony most of the other people in the ceremony were on their knees with me. The energy was amazing! It even brought the batteries in my friend's camcorder up to full charge*!

During the ceremonies the clouds formed a perfect image of a white bird that most witnesses described as a dove. (The dove is one of the symbols of the Holy Spirit.) We also saw a double rainbow, which, from many parts of west Sedona, seemed to touch down at the Shrine where the ceremony took place. Everyone who noticed these things was certain they were a sign from Spirit.

GROUP CONSCIOUSNESS AND CEREMONY

As a society, one of the most important concepts we need to come to terms with is group consciousness, and the fact that the combined mental energies of all humanity create the psychic atmosphere of our planet.

As part of the evolutionary process of our planet, groups of light-workers need to come together and perform ceremonies that send Universal Love and positive mental images of peace, life, and joy into the planetary energy grid. (Our group consciousness is an aspect of the planetary energy grid.)

The meditations and ceremonies in this book, particularly the Medicine Wheel/Merkaba, are provided by Spirit to be our tools. With these tools we can greatly increase the power of small groups and be truly effective in getting into the energy level of existence where the energies of the group consciousness reside.

In regarding the concept of group consciousness it is important to realize that a very large portion of the negative and undesirable things that happen come into being because these events are being fueled by negative and distorted thought-energy and the emotional energies of hate and fear. This creates a type of "closed loop" system that has the potential to create more situations that lead to the creation of more undesirable psychic energy. Breaking this cycle, through the use of ceremony and the invocation of Universal Love, is one of the most important things we can do.

---

* I am serious when I say that it appeared that the batteries in Mr. Edwin Serrano's video camera did in fact come up to full charge during the ceremony.

DID THE 1992 MOUNT SHASTA ASCENSION CELEBRATION
PREVENT A MAJOR EARTHQUAKE?

The concept of controlling planetary destiny with prayer and ceremony is an idea whose time has come. More people need to begin taking responsibility for organizing ascension groups and ceremonies. Each region needs to create events. Make it fun and make it pay. World peace and healing ceremonies should be promoted like any other type of outdoor event, such as a rock concert or sporting event.

Let us examine, as an example of an event for which a fee was charged, the Mount Shasta ascension celebration that took place September 17-20, 1992. If the people who promoted this event had not been able to charge a fee, there would have been no ascension celebration. And if there had not been an ascension celebration, there might have been a catastrophic earthquake in California.

As you may remember, during the summer of 1992 southern California was struck by a series of powerful earthquakes, and it was widely suspected by scientists, psychics, and the general public that a devastating earthquake was imminent. Yet, as of the writing of these words, almost three years have passed and most of California remains relatively unscathed. Could this have anything to do with group consciousness?

The Harmonic Convergence II ceremony on July 26, 1992, took place just before the most powerful California earthquake of 1992. As soon as this quake occurred, various psychics began predicting that a major earthquake would hit California within a week of the 26th of July. Fortunately, this did not occur. Later that summer, however, several prominent seismologists and a group of psychics who work with the University of California once again began predicting that a big earthquake would occur early in the autumn season of 1992.

The ascension celebration at Mt. Shasta took place right before autumn began, and we can now note that the entire season passed without a major earthquake. Did these ceremonies counteract the earthquakes that had been predicted by scientists and psychics alike? Some psychics within the research group believe that the ceremony at Mount Shasta did indeed nullify the energy of the earthquakes they had foreseen.

As a final note on the concept of using group consciousness to control planetary destiny, let us consider the effect psychic predictions may or may not have on the manifestation of natural disasters. Do the various predictions of disaster create a psychic atmosphere that will ultimately result in our combined mental energies creating a disaster, *or do these predictions provide us with images of possible futures that we cancel before they become manifest?*

The information in this book can be put to use anywhere on this planet, as the energy of Spirit is universal. Nonetheless, many of you will feel drawn to Sedona and will want to experience the powers of the red rocks and the Vortices. My advice for people who come here to explore this path is as follows: come with the intention of performing the spiritual exercises in this book; I am certain you will get results.

Remember that the energy of a meditation ceremony or invocation can last for years, so don't blow your visit by lounging around a tourist trap. Instead, concentrate the energy of your visit on using the boost of the Vortices to help you invoke Spirit for help, guidance, and protection. Most other goals are secondary to what can be accomplished by performing certain spiritual exercises and meditations in a Vortex area.

A lot of people wonder what Sedona is all about, and a lot of people leave here still wondering. In fact, many of the people who live here do not seem to be quite getting it either. The information in this book will help change that. Sedona is not coffee shops, health food stores, or gift shops; these things are to be found everywhere. Sedona is the land of enchantment. To understand this, you must "tune in" to the energies the land provides, and then use these energies to increase the power of your prayers and ceremonies.

My study of metaphysics and shamanism has shown me that one of the most important things that you can do to accelerate your spiritual evolution is to use the Pillar of Light, as detailed in this book, to access your Higher Self and your Soul (which is a higher aspect of the Higher Self).

Making your connection to your Higher Self is important to your personal evolution, as this aspect of your being has a direct connection with the superconscious realms of the Soul and the I AM presence of the Universal Mind. The energies of the ascension come to us through the Pillar of Light and the Higher Self/Soul.

If you are interested in working with Angels, Guides, or Masters, or Angelic entities, it is important to understand that the primary reason you would want to invoke one of these entities is for assistance in accessing your Higher Self.

When asking for assistance from an Angel, Guide, or Master it is important to qualify your prayer/invocations with statements such as, "I ask for an entity who serves the Lord God Creator of the universe and who works for the positive evolution of humanity in harmony with the Brotherhoods of Light."

It is also important to note that I am not asking that you **give up your body** or your *Will* to any other entity. Wise mystics do not invite alien entities into themselves. Possession by an extraterrestrial is neither glamorous nor desirable, in spite of what the "walk-ins" might say.

Once you begin to perform your ceremonies for invoking your Higher Self and your Angelic guide, you will be putting powerful forces in motion that will help take you where you want to go, as long as you are willing to keep doing the work. Please remember that your ceremonial invocations of these Universal Forces can have effects that last for years. This is serious business that puts you in contact with tremendous powers that can vastly improve your life.

When in Sedona, just about any place where you may find yourself is a good place for a ceremony or meditation. Here is a short commentary on a few of the more notable power spots in Sedona: The **Red Rock Crossing/Cathedral Rock** area for clearing the aura and invoking Angels; **Bell Rock** for the Pillar of Light and the Antahkarana; **Airport Vortex** for the Pillar of Light and the Antahkarana; and **Boynton Canyon** and **Cathedral Rock** for inner plane work or contact with Angels. Please remember that you do not have to be in Sedona for these ceremonies to work. Ascension is a planetary phenomenon. You can call on Spirit from anywhere.

It is interesting to note that many of the rock spires in the Sedona area are natural energy channels for spiritual energy between the Earth and the stars. Therefore, the closer one is to a vertical formation, the easier it is to pick up information and/or energy from the higher intelligences. Boynton Canyon and Fay Canyon have excellent power spots near their parking areas; just look for the rock spires. **Please remember to protect plant life in these areas by staying on the trails, and please, do not pick branches off trees for "offerings." Quiet is also appreciated at these areas.**

The area directly to the north of the back gate of the resort in Boynton Canyon is also an excellent area in which to perform your ceremonies. When you get to this area you will find that there are several clearings adjacent to the trail that will serve you quite well. At Long Canyon, the most popular power spot is known as Rachel's Hill and is located at the end of Long Canyon Road. (Parking below.)

After you find a place where you feel comfortable and you have settled down, I suggest that you begin meditating as you visualize yourself in a Pillar of Light as described in the meditation section. This Pillar of Light will serve both to shield you and to carry spiritual energy back and forth between you and the higher realms.

Once the Pillar of Light has been established, your prayers and invocations will be more effective. My best advice for projecting telepathic messages to the higher realms is to believe that it can be done, and will it to be so. As you do this, concentrate on the power centers in your head: the crown, third eye, and the chamber in the center of the brain. Visualize yourself surrounded with Light and allow your thoughts to become one with that Light. Call out to your Higher Self and the Angels with both your thoughts and your voice. (After you have spoken your prayers you can switch to nonverbal telepathic communication; just think loud!)

If you want to contact a spirit guide, ask that the universe send you a guide. If you want to work with the Angels, invoke them. If you want help, guidance, and protection, ask for these things. But do not expect to see spaceships or to meet alien entities in their physical forms. The entities I consider to be most benevolent operate in higher nonphysical dimensions.

Please remember to qualify all your invocations with words such as: "In the name of the Creator of Love" – or – "I seek guidance from entities that serve the office of the Christ and positive human evolution in the ever-expanding life system of the universe."

UNDERSTANDING THE UNIVERSAL LAWS OF CAUSE AND EFFECT

Metaphysics is an ancient scientific philosophy that has been studied by all great philosophers, theologians, and scientists throughout history. It has only been in recent times, however, that these teachings have separated from the mainstream establishment churches in the Western world and begun proclaiming a more complete understanding of that which we call God.

Metaphysics itself is a clearly defined and highly respectable field of scientific philosophy that has been practiced by wise men, scientists and theologians throughout history. In fact, the study of metaphysics has been the basis for the scientific philosophies of many of history's well-known thinkers, including Plato, Aristotle, Pythagoras, Sir Isaac Newton and Professor Albert Einstein.

The deeds and beliefs of these great minds should be sufficient to demonstrate to all that metaphysical philosophy and the science of metaphysics represent valid fields of study for those who wish to understand the ultimate truths of existence. But it is particularly interesting and ironic to note that Harvard University has recently released Sir Isaac Newton's personal diary, which clearly states that he studied the Kabbalah, which he referred to as "Egyptian metaphysics."

The irony here is that, not only is Sir Isaac Newton the "father" of many important scientific theories, practices, and the mathematic descriptions of quantum mechanics, he is also considered to be the founder of the school of thought known as "scientific materialism." It is this popular school of thought that is primarily responsible for promoting the theory that the universe is dead matter and that human consciousness is merely a chemical reaction in the brain. The irony here is that Master Newton obviously had a firm belief in the inherently living nature of the universe, and if he could be with us today he would be thoroughly dismayed by the inherently agnostic nature of many of today's scientists.

In rethinking the legitimacy of metaphysical thought it is also interesting to note the work of Professor Albert Einstein. While he never professed to be a metaphysician, his works indicate that he had a profound intuitive knowledge of advanced metaphysical principles. In fact, in our modern era Professor Albert Einstein stands out as one of the greatest metaphysicians of all time, as he not only revolutionized the science of physics and mankind's view of the nature of reality, but also because he based all of his theories on "the observer."

This is because Professor Einstein was acutely aware of the fact that all things in the universe are based on the subjective experience of the individual, the "I Am" observer. Like all great minds, Albert Einstein came to the very metaphysical, very magical, very shamanic realization that nothing matters except that which is within the field of individual experience. It is as Don Juan said to Carlos Castaneda, "Each person experiences a separate reality." What this means is all that matters to the individual are those things that directly affect their awareness. The final result of this philosophy is the belief that through the application of the "Metaphysical Laws" individual humans can create any reality they choose.

One can easily imagine that the world would be a much better place if more people were ready to accept the fact that they can control their own lives through the application of Metaphysical Laws, and fortunately, it seems that people are waking up to this fact on a grand scale. Suddenly, here in America and in many other countries, a lot of people are beginning to show signs that our species is becoming evolved to the point where we are ready to grasp at the infinite.

As for the word "metaphysics" itself, we find that this phrase originated during the time of ancient Greece. According to the Encyclopedia Britannica the literal translation of the word metaphysics is: "What comes after physics." This translation seems to miss the mark a bit, and I will suggest that we instead think of metaphysics as "what is beyond physical reality." In relation to this it should be noted that the early Aristotelians also referred to metaphysics as "the first philosophy," which is, of course, the study of God as the nature of the universe.

It is also interesting to know what the Greek roots of the word *philosophy* are: *philos* and *sophos*. *Philos* meaning love, and *sophos* meaning knowledge. The word *"sophos"* is derived from the name of the Goddess of Wisdom, Sophia. Therefore, the philosopher is a "lover of wisdom."

Today, metaphysics is recognized on the university level as a legitimate, well-defined scientific philosophy of attempting to understand the nature of the universe. Nonetheless, the parameters and meanings of "metaphysics" are widely misunderstood by just about everyone who has not had formal training in the actual science of metaphysics. To clarify our terms, I will state that at our current level of language use in our society there is a large difference between the words "metaphysical" and "metaphysics."

The word "metaphysical" can denote anything that has to do with phenomena coming in from, or associated with, the nonphysical realm, including the quantum forces of subatomic physics. Metaphysical phenomena can include many things that people in the consciousness movement may be interested in, including all psychic phenomena such as ESP, channeling (mediumship), psychic reading (fortune-telling) and out-of-body experiences such as astral projection. Many people, including those who are interested in Native American teachings or the teachings of Don Juan, may refer to the metaphysical realm as "Spirit."

Metaphysics as a scientific philosophy of the application of Spiritual Laws of cause and effect can be said to include magic or any form of reality control, such as shamanism or advanced Native American teachings, as well as certain aspects of meditation, yoga, astrology, hands-on healing, and all other things that involve "Spirit," or the metaphysical God-forces that create reality.

There are two main branches of metaphysics: speculative and practical (otherwise known as philosophical and scientific). These two aspects of metaphysics are, however, in no way mutually exclusive. And while a student of metaphysical philosophy may never become deeply involved in the scientific application of metaphysics, a metaphysician who is also involved in the scientific application of metaphysical principles will always have an understanding of metaphysical philosophy. This book is primarily concerned with the practice, or scientific aspects, of metaphysics in relation to elevating the consciousness, increasing the vibrational state of the body, and consciously creating reality.

17

To understand the science of metaphysics the student must accept the fact that there is no separation between the individual and the universe, and that the universe is a unified whole in which all seemingly individual units experience existence as aspects of the greater unity. Taking this a bit further, we find that as a consciousness entity each human being has the potential to operate as a self-realized co-creator with the Universal Mind. The implications of this are, of course, somewhat beyond the Earth-bound comprehension of the materialists, the agnostics, and those who do not philosophize.

A classic study of the science of metaphysics involves the understanding and use of what are commonly referred to as Metaphysical Laws or Universal Laws. I have found that I prefer to refer to the Metaphysical Laws as Universal Truth Principles, because the word "law" has been misused and maligned in our society to the point that it has developed many negative connotations.

The interpretation of the Metaphysical Laws, or Universal Truth Principles, is, of course, open to a great deal of philosophical debate. In this discourse, however, we will not engage in much debate over these principles; instead we will move forward and explore my interpretations of the basic Metaphysical Truth Principles as they were taught to me.

In exploring these Universal Truth Principles we must understand that they are philosophical interpretations of the workings of the Universal Mind, the I AM, and therefore **these principles define the mechanics of the universe itself**. When the student understands these principles they can use them to interpret their experiences on their life path, and perhaps more importantly use these principles to create realities that are in more perfect harmony with the Source of all things, and therefore more nurturing and enjoyable.

The understanding and application of these principles represents the basis for all forms of reality control in high magic, mysticism, and shamanism. Perhaps the most notable difference between the modern metaphysics of Soul Star teachings and the practice of magic or shamanism is that we do not usually work with spirits or lesser gods, preferring to go directly to The Source: GOD.

LOVE – LIGHT – LIFE

Learned metaphysicians interpret the primary aspects of the Universal Mind as Love, Light, and Life. As simplistic and *New Agey* as this might sound, this belief system is both profound in its implications, and ancient and proven to be true by metaphysical philosophers of all eras.

To understand metaphysics is to understand the universe. The universe is Life and Light, created and sustained by Love, and all things that we can comprehend are parts of the unified whole of the universe. There is no separation between man and nature; all are ONE. The universe is filled with Life and Light which continuously strive to expand, multiply, and diversify. The program for Universal Life and the accompanying will for self-preservation is evident in all things. Even rocks can be seen to have an existence as living beings when it is understood that "dead" matter is alive within the body of the universe.

LOVE, as a consciousness program for Universal Creation, manifests as unity, harmony and joy in nature. Understanding the unifying nature of Love is an important aspect of metaphysical philosophy: God is Love. To express Love in

18

one's heart and life is to be in harmony with the universe and the highest universal principles. When a student achieves Christ Consciousness they are in complete harmony with all things and beyond duality. Love is the strength of the universe. The Universal Love of God sustains all Light and Life in the universe, and all things in the universe know the Love of God through the **joy of existence.**

In the study of sacred geometry the metaphysician sees Love as the "consciousness program" of the Universal Mind which unifies all things. It is as many great scientists have said: "There appears to be a unifying principle in nature that operates in an intelligent manner." The metaphysician sees this as the Universal Mind in action.

Beyond the discussion of the philosophical ideas associated with Love, learned metaphysicians know that we all experience well-defined and easily recognizable energies that are known to be aspects of the Threefold Flame of Universal Love, Life, and Light. In the various schools these aspect of **Universal Life-Force Energies** are commonly referred to as chi, ki, Kundalini, Prana, and reiki. Love as an energy is also known to create an emotional/energy response which is referred to as "Ananda," or joy.

The orgasm is a well-known effect of the energies we refer to as Universal Love, Life and Light. When a human reaches sexual climax, each cell in their physical body temporarily opens up to a heightened state of conductivity to Universal Love, Life, and Light that carry the very noticeable energy frequencies of the emotions we call bliss and joy (Ananda). Sexual energy is often spoken of as "the first initiation" into the mysteries of nonphysical universal creation. Students of metaphysics or yoga, at some point during their training, should have the opportunity to learn how to control or *work* with the energy of the orgasm to either prolong the effect or achieve highly desirable advanced states of consciousness. (Read on.)

It must also be understood that while it is a scientific fact that the bodily sensations of the orgasm are on the physical level the direct result of various hormones released by the glands, yogis and metaphysicians know that these hormones are the secondary effect of life-force energy that is brought more fully into the body during the act of "making" Love. This energy not only stimulates each cell of the physical body, it also stimulates various glands in the body, which then secrete hormones that both increase the effect of bodily pleasure and help ground these energies into the physical structure of the body.

Soul Star instruction is designed to teach the student to achieve states of energy in the body that are highly energized with Love, Life, and Light. These energy states are often accompanied by energetic tingling on the skin, a sense of increased vibration in the body, and, on occasion, the sensation of a cool fire running through the body, cleansing, purifying, healing, and *reprogramming* the body/mind. Soul Star meditations such as this are done with prayer, invocation, the *Will*, visualization and the breath. Private sessions also include inner plane/Higher Self work and initiation with symbols.

Soul Star training involves attuning the physical body/mind to the Higher Self through the use of Universal Love, Life and Light. When summoned, these energies purify the mind and body, thereby making the student a suitable vehicle for the Soul on the physical plane.

19

The existence of Universal Love is somewhat more difficult to prove to the uninitiated than the existence of Universal Light and Life. While Light and Life are self-evident, we find that Love manifests as a decidedly more transcendental quality that is difficult if not impossible to isolate or quantify as a "metaphysical energy" on any type of laboratory equipment that I know of. It is because of this fact that many establishment scientists as well as agnostics and atheists deny that Love is a universal quality, or that Love has anything at all to do with the formation of the universe.

The denial or acceptance of Universal Love represents a primary departure between the philosophies of the materialists and those who believe in the existence of God. This dichotomy also represents an aspect of the most profound question that any human can ponder: Are we merely the product of chance evolution in a universe of dead matter, or are we aspects of a greater, Divine Being? Whatever the case, belief in either philosophy represents an act of faith.

When attempting to prove whether Love exists as a universal force beyond the subjective reality of our individual minds, we must be willing to admit that at this point there is no scientifically verifiable proof. The belief in Universal Love is somewhat of an act of faith, because Love can only be detected within the body, by the senses.

Nonetheless, every spiritual master, channeled entity or school of mysticism that has any notable lineage or reputation says that Love is the force that creates and unifies all things. And that faith is the quality we need to cultivate in order to understand the Truth of Universal Love.

Following this line of thought a little further, we find that according to the teachings of the Master Christ, Love is an aspect of the Holy Spirit. To an Earth-bound human the Holy Spirit represents the mystery of mysteries, the ultimate power of creation that emanates directly from the Godhead. In light of this it is also interesting to note that in the original Greek and Aramaic languages of the New Testament the phrase that is translated as Holy Spirit, could be more properly translated as "Holy Breath." The Holy Spirit breathes Life into all things. The Holy Spirit is Universal Life Force Energy.

Love is the primal element of creation that works in harmony with Light and Life to create all the universes of the universe. Love cannot be quantified by Earth-bound humans, it is a transcendental concept that must be accepted as an act of faith and experienced within the body and mind. Therefore, we are taught that the best thing we can do in relation to the Holy Spirit is to honor It and consciously encourage It to flow through us at all times.

In metaphysical philosophy it is understood that there are two primary forms of Love: conditional love and universal (or unconditional) Love. Conditional love is a strictly subjective experience that occurs within the mind of the individual; it is a form of attachment, desire and judgment. Therefore, in the Buddhistic sense, conditional love is very much a part of the transitory world of illusions.

Universal Love is the basic quality of the primal God-force that creates all things. In its simplest definition, Love is the **Will** to create. It is the directive of the first thought produced by the Universal Mind: "Let there be Light."

Universal Light is therefore an aspect of Universal Love. It carries the program of Love throughout the universe. In metaphysical meditations, the meditator, through an act of *Will*, and under the guidance of a human teacher or Master such as Christ, learns how to attune themselves to the pure Love-Light of the Universal Creator. Universal Light is also known to be the primary manifestation of all Life in the universe. This includes Light itself, both spiritual and physical, as well as all matter, stars, planets, as well as biological and pure energy life forms.

In regarding this we must also understand that the ancients equated the soul of the human with the energy of the stars. This is why this course of instruction is called Soul Star. It is no accident that the Latin word for the Sun is Sol. Each one of us is an aspect of the Love, Light, and Life of the Creator of all things, the entity that the Master Christ referred to in his native language as "Abba," or Father. **The energy that creates stars is the energy that creates souls.** To activate the Body of Light/Merkaba is to merge the physical body with the Higher Self, which is an aspect of the body of universal consciousness: the Soul.

Universal Love is the *Will* to create, and then nurture (sustain) all life. Love is seen to be the most primal and important aspect of God. Love is Universal Life and Light in action. And the universe experiences joy in the realization of its own existence.

The universe applies the Law of Love in its continuous expansion, multiplication, and diversification. Love is the primal element of creation that creates all the universes of universes. Love cannot be quantified by Earth-bound humans. It is a transcendental concept that must be accepted as an act of faith and experienced within the body and mind. Therefore, we are taught that the best thing we can do in relation to the Holy Spirit is to honor It and consciously encourage It to flow though us at all times.

The natural product of Universal Love in action is the desire for self-preservation. The desire and command to preserve Life is seen as the primary Truth in the universe. For humans the Universal Law of self-preservation manifests in four primary ways: the desire to preserve our individual lives, the desire to experience life as joy, the desire to create offspring (or to simply create), and the desire to achieve a continuation of our consciousness beyond the Earth realm in the ever-expanding life systems of the universe. This process is known as ascension. Christians refer to ascension as "everlasting life," the ultimate form of self-preservation.

This brings us to one of the most important teachings of religion and metaphysical philosophy: All life is an aspect of the One we call God, the Universal Creator. Therefore we should remember to treat all life with respect, and treat our fellow humans as we would ourselves. This is Christ Consciousness in action.

A common thread woven through all schools of metaphysical philosophy is the concept of "Logos." The word Logos denotes the creative power of the Universal Mind. This word comes to us from the ancient Greeks and in its most literal sense Logos means "word." The power of "the word," or language, has been recognized in all schools of philosophy and spirituality as being the ultimate concept that any individual is capable of comprehending, because all things within the individual field of awareness within each person's mind are expressed as the dialogue of self-awareness, or language.

The primary reason that the metaphysician, the mystic, the magician, or the shaman needs to be aware of the all-encompassing implications of language is that it is through language that each individual interfaces with the Universal Mind; that to control language is to control reality: I speak, therefore I am.

The control of reality/experience through the understanding of the use of language is a vast subject that can only be learned in stages. At this point let it suffice to say that meditating on the reality of awareness itself is an excellent exercise. It is very empowering to realize that the "I Am" within each one of us is an aspect of the greater I AM that is the universe, and that there is no part of our being which is not part of the universe. All are One!

As such, we find that a basic principle of metaphysical philosophy is that, as an inseparable aspect of the infinite universe, there is no reason why any human should be limited in any way, and that the only reason we are limited is because we limit ourselves with faulty beliefs about the nature of reality. To overcome this students must erase many "programs" that they have accepted from social training. And they must find new ways to language the *image* of reality that they wish to attain. At this point I feel that for modern Americans the best techniques for re-imaging reality are those of the various schools of Neurolinguistic Programming. (I feel a particular affinity to Tad James' Advanced Neuro Dynamics, as he is also a fellow student of Hawaiian shamanism.*)

Mind is a concept that is inseparable from language. Mind expresses itself through language, and it must be realized that self-awareness cannot be accomplished without language.

Language is not, however, the exclusive realm of dialogue as it appears within our minds. Language includes all concepts of which a human can be aware: Earth-bound, spiritual, and transcendental. Therefore, language should be understood to have a very large definition, that can even be said to be multidimensional.

As a demonstration of this we must realize that all forms of energy contain information and therefore, language is energy. The structuring of the energies that compose the universe can be expressed as a language of mathematics and geometry that are imprinted on the basic energetic force of the universe as a whole. This is the psychological structure of the Mind of God.

* Advanced Neuro Dynamics Inc. 1833 Kalakua Ave. #908 Honolulu, Hawaii 96815

In the application of metaphysics the student needs to understand that every-thing is energy, and that through the basic energies that create our universe our minds interface with all things. For proof of this we can look at Professor Einstein's work and the theories of quantum physics. And as all energy contains information, we can see that energy itself is a form of language. Einstein also correctly theorized that the universe is a "unified field" of energy. Taking this a step further, meta-physical schools speak of the universe itself as the Universal Mind. This denotes the fact that the universe itself is a self-aware entity which expresses itself as awareness in energy, form, and Life.

The classic teaching is that the Universal Mind expresses itself in a language that manifests as the creation of all things. In contemplating this we are reminded of the words of St. John in the New Testament: "In the beginning was the Word, and the Word was with God, and the Word was God." And does not the very word "world" come from the root – word? All that is, is Language.

In application, to control the language dialogue within our consciousness is to control the way we perceive reality; for in fact, each individual consciousness-en-tity creates their own universe within their own mind. Each individual knows only what they perceive. So it must be understood that all things that are perceived exist as language within the mind; language is the vehicle of perception. The implica-tions of this are profound. All great philosophers, scientists, seers, mystics, and magicians know of this concept and work with it in their own ways. The lan-guage/perception equation is the key to all things.

The most important concept to be aware of in this discussion (or anything else, for that matter) is that everything in the known universe is based on the observa-tions of the observer (the I Am within each of us). Einstein and Don Juan were acutely aware of this. Einstein said that "Everything is relative to the position of the observer," and Don Juan said that each person experiences a "separate reality." (And all observations and pictures of reality are structured in language.)

For the sake of clarity it must be understood that language is not the exclusive realm of dialogue as it appears within the human mind. Not only does language include all concepts of which a human can be aware of – Earth-bound, spiritual, and transcendental, language (apparently) also involves Universal Mind concepts that are completely beyond the realm of human perception or speculation. There-fore, language should be understood to have a very large definition that can even be said to be multidimensional.

We must also realize that all forms of energy contain information, and there-fore, language is an aspect of energy. The structuring of the energies that compose the universe are interpreted by human observers as a dialogue of mathematics, geometry and harmony. When considering the higher aspects of universal crea-tion, mathematics, geometry, and harmony are seen as the foundations for the manifestation of the human experience on any dimension, and that which we call mathematics, geometry and harmony are constructs created by the Universal Mind which produce the orderly formation of the Love, Light, and Life in the manifestation of All That Is.

The reality that our mind perceives appears to be built from physical objects. Upon investigation, however, we find that while it is difficult to scientifically isolate or quantify the existence of nonphysical (or metaphysical) forces such as life force energy or universal consciousness, it can nonetheless be demonstrated that in-depth deductive and scientific analysis of physical reality reveals a great deal of evidence that seems to indicate that there is an *informing principle* or *intelligence*, evident in all natural phenomena. It is this informing principle that metaphysicians refer to as the Universal Mind.

In metaphysics the existence of the Universal Mind is taken to be a basic fact. The universe is not believed to be made of dead matter with no intelligent motivation; it is instead taught that the universe is a living, self-aware entity. The unified field of energy that is the universe is Love, Life and Light. The universe does not create matter, stars, starlight, planets, and life by mere chance. It is instead a self-aware entity that consciously creates a myriad of multidimensional realities.

From the human perspective, mathematics and geometry form the basic patternings of the primal energy that creates our reality. Each atom of our body is a waveform conceived according to perfect unified principles that evidently hold true in all regions of the known universe. The Universal Mind is everywhere, creating, informing, and empowering all things with Love, Light, and Life.

When contemplating the reality of the Universal Mind we must realize that mind is a principle that is inseparable from language. Consciousness is impossible to achieve without dialogue: "I think therefore I am," and so forth. It is from the understanding of these concepts that the ancient Greek philosophers began using the term "Logos" (which means "word") to describe the Creator of all things. It is also interesting to note that the principle of Logos, or the creative word, was recognized by the apostle John: "In the beginning was the Word, and the Word was with God, and the Word was God."

It should come as no surprise that the word "God" itself has an interesting connection to the study of metaphysics. The word God is a derivative of the Hebrew letter Yod, which is "Y" in English. The letter Yod is symbolic of the flame, and in its written form it actually resembles a curling flame, (or dare I say a spiraling Vortex of fire?) The flame symbolized by Yod has a great deal of significance. It is symbolic of the primal energy that creates all things, the divine fire that illuminates all creation with the sacred Light which carries forth the Wisdom and *Will* of the Creator of All Things.

The flame symbolized by the letter Yod is also symbolic of the inherently masculine nature of the primal God-force that stretches forth to impregnate the primal void. It is Love, Light, and Life. The flame is also symbolic of the lingam, and it is from the linguistic root lingam that we get the modern English word "language." Language, in its highest meaning denotes the creative power of the Universal Mind, the Logos, or God. For in reality these three words define exactly the same thing.

The Yod, or lingam, represents the singular nature of the Godhead which enters into the universes of creation as the threefold flame of Love, Light, and Life. It is because of their direct connection to the Godhead that Love, Light, and Life are known to be absolute Universal Truths. It is from this awareness that metaphysicians have discovered the Universal Truth Principle: "*Light is Truth.*"

In application, *Light is Truth* tells us that The Light (or energy) that emanates directly from the Mind of God is known to be the pure essence of the Ultimate Truth of existence. Therefore, when humans consciously begin working with "The Light" they become illuminated with the absolute Truth of the Universal Mind, which is expressed in the Language of Light. This pure energy from the Great Central Sun has the ability to transcend third-dimensional blockages and thereby re-imprint the student with the higher Light codes of pure Love that automatically cleanse and purify our bodies of energy blockages and negative mental conditions, such as the "big three "sin, guilt, and fear.

When working with Light, the student must be aware that many schools of spiritual thought teach that Light can also be used by entities who do not have humanity's best interest in mind. Therefore, if we desire protection from negative forces we must remember to qualify our spiritual work with invocations of the Master Jesus Christ, the avatar of the true New Age.

Qualifying energy is one of the most important parts of this work. It is therefore suggested that at the beginning of each meditation or ceremony you pray out loud and ask that only entities who serve the Creator of Love and eternal life and who work for the *positive evolution of humanity* respond to your prayers.

As a daily routine or at least a few times a week it is also beneficial to meditate on the reality of the being we call Jesus Christ, who was known in his time as Joshua or Eshua Ben Joseph (Joshua, son of Joseph). As an aid to this we may use pictures of Jesus, but we must realize that these pictures are like a map; they are only representations of the real thing. No one that I know of is certain what Jesus looked like, although we may have a reliable guide for this in the image found on the Shroud of Turin.

Is this the real Jesus?

This photograph is a colorized version of the original image on The Shroud of Turin.

It was colorized by the Master Sai Baba. According to witnesses he simply passed his hand over a black and white photograph and produced this image that has more detail and open eyes. The eyes and hair are brown.

Ascension, for humanity, is the process of releasing three-dimensional distortions through the purification of the physical, mental, and spiritual bodies. As these consciousness vehicles (bodies) are brought into alignment with the Universal Truth Principles, their energy/vibration levels will increase until they pass the threshold limitation of this dimension, thereby making a quantum jump into the next higher octave of existence.

Various sources of information, including the *Keys of Enoch* and Drunvalo Melchizedek, tell us that the ascension process will take us into the high overtones of the fourth dimension for a short sojourn that will result in our attainment of fifth-dimensional existence.

At these higher levels, our consciousness vehicle experiences the Universal Christ Consciousness of the Soul and we will gain access to our complete multidimensional, multi-lifetime memory as an imperishable unit in the ever-expanding life system of the universe.

In these fourth and fifth-dimensional realities, thought instantly manifests as reality. Therefore, only entities that are *clear* will be able to maintain themselves in these higher realms. To be clear is to be beyond the three-dimensional distortions of sin, guilt, fear, and duality-consciousness. To become clear is to align oneself with the highest Universal Truth Principles: Love, Life, and Light.

ASCENSION AS A TEST?

Interestingly enough, it seems that one of the primary tests of ascension is not whether we are is obedient to the entities we sometimes refer to as "gods," but whether we will accept responsibility for ourselves as sovereign entities within the universe and simply say NO to entities who seek to control humanity with illusions of guilt, sin, and fear, accepting responsibility as sovereign free-will beings who create reality for ourselves. The paradox within the paradox is that the lesser gods who demand obedience and inflict pain also appear to be our teachers of ultimate freedom.

"Ye shall obey my commands, no matter how unreasonable they may be, and you will do so till the day when you become brave and powerful enough to say no to me. At that point you will become qualified to take control of your own destiny."

The information given in *The Keys of Enoch* serves as a bridge between the Infinite Mind of God and the minds of humanity. The information given in the *Keys* transcends everything the common Earthling has been taught. It is the teaching for our age; it is the ultimate manual for the ascension.*

The *Book of Knowledge: The Keys of Enoch*, published and taught by **the Academy for Future Science**, is one of the most unique books in the planetary library. Dare we allow ourselves to believe that *The Keys of Enoch* is in fact exactly what it claims to be: a direct communication from the highest celestial hierarchy, delivered to this planet by the Angelic orders of Metatron, Michael, Melchizedek, and Enoch under the direction of the Source Creator of all things?

In the introduction to *The Keys of Enoch*, Dr. J.J. Hurtak makes the declaration that he was given the *Keys* during an experience wherein he was taken before the Throne of God by an interdimensional light vehicle known as a Merkaba. Dr. Hurtak does not claim to be the author of the *Keys*, instead, he states that the *Keys of Enoch* are the creation of one of the aspects of the Godhead called Metatron.

The Keys of Enoch is therefore, *Metatronic science*, providing "the disciplines to create and completely restore life systems of creation in the outer universes." *The Keys of Enoch* refers to Metatron as "the visible manifestation of The Deity." Metatron is the Logos, the Creator of the Divine Word. In Hebrew, Metatron is called El Shaddai.

Upon examining *The Keys of Enoch*, it becomes difficult to imagine that they are the product of Dr. Hurtak's imagination. *The Keys* are complex, scientific, and detailed. They provide interesting and plausible explanations to our big questions, such as, what is the nature of God, how God creates the universe of universes, how and why human beings were created, and why, in spite of the fact that we are told that God is infinitely wise and loving, there is hate, anger, and disharmony.

Dare we allow ourselves to imagine that *The Keys of Enoch* is truly a direct communication from God? Why not? *The Keys* certainly do not tell us to do anything most of us would consider to be bad. In fact, the *Keys* encourage us to take a deeper look at the teachings of the Master Christ and the Old Testament. Dr. Hurtak informs us that *The Keys of Enoch* was brought to us at this time because our planet is indeed in a time of transformation that will take us beyond all of our current definitions of reality and that we are in fact being retrieved by the celestial hierarchies and rescued from the distortion of existence in the outer universe.

The Keys of Enoch offers humanity a scientific and religious understanding of this process. It can be understood in its simplest terms as working with the feminine aspect of divinity, the Holy Spirit (Shekinah), in establishing a Pillar of Spiritual Light around the body that forms a bridge between the physical aspects of the body/mind and the Christ Overself (Atman – Soul), which is focused in the ninth chakra.

---

* Available through the Academy for Future Science, P.O. Box FE, Los Gatos, California, 95031

The Keys of Enoch is based upon the science of understanding language as the structure of reality. Everything we can know exists as language. Consciousness is language. Without the dialogue of self-reflection, consciousness cannot exist. Language/consciousness originates from the Universal Logos, Metatron, as the Master "I AM" Threshold Commands. Consider this classic metaphysical formula given to us in the New Testament: "In the beginning was the Word, and the Word was with God, and the Word was God."

The Infinite Mind of God expresses itself with pure energy emissions, the "Living Language of Light." This Language of Light exists on all levels of creation from subatomic to cosmic, organizing the Holy Spirit, Shekinah, into the harmonic structure of the universe. Language creates the patterns that create reality.

The Language of Living Light functions as the bridge between our limited third-dimensional minds and Universal God-consciousness. The highest level of mystical knowledge is the understanding of language as the structure of reality. To have total control of the use of language in speech and thought is to have total control of reality (see the teachings of Don Juan). Language is energy, and all energy is a form of language (see Jose Argüelles' *The Mayan Factor*). Language creates and connects all facets of the universal energy matrix. The study of sacred geometry is one aspect of understanding the universal Language of Light.

In the three-dimensional reality of planet Earth, the language that comes closest to expressing the true Language of Light is Hebrew. Key 305:22 tells us that "The sacred Language is thoughts of God." – Key 215:63 tells us, "In essence the flame scriptures (*of Hebrew*) were composed out of living geometries of God's Word, extended to connect with the vibratory resonance grids of the Earth."

DIVINE ATTUNEMENT and DIVINE PROTECTION:

KODOISH, KODOISH, KODOISH, ADONAI 'TSEBAYOTH

"Metatron also explained to me that the salutation Kodoish, Kodoish, Kodoish, Adonai 'Tsebayoth should be used to discern the spiritual from the negative forces. In fact, this salutation is so strong that negative forces cannot remain for any length of time in the presence of its vibration." (Key 305:42)

Key 305 of *The Keys of Enoch* tells us that the mantra "**Kodoish, Kodoish, Kodoish, Adonai 'Tsebayoth,**" (Holy, Holy, Holy, Lord God of Hosts) is "the measure and cycle of all states of matter/radiation," and that it creates resonance between all levels of creation and the primary Source Creator. Those of you who are familiar with the New Testament's Book of Revelation and the vision of St. John will recognize "Holy, Holy, Holy, Lord God of Hosts" as the mantra the four entities surrounding the throne of God chant.

The Keys of Enoch states that "Kodoish, Kodoish, Kodoish, Adonai 'Tsebayoth" ties all rhythms of the body together with the spiritual rhythms of the Overself. When we chant this mantra, our Christ Overself bodies are quickened into direct work with the physical body. It is suggested this mantra be incorporated into our daily meditation practices, as it is known to be the most important key to divine attunement. (Key 305:7,26,28,36)

We transform our bodies and activate our Merkabas by attuning ourselves to the Universal Life Force Energies that emanate from the Throne of God. This process of attunement energizes and purifies every particle of energy that makes up the body. It is suggested that this entire section on ascension yoga be read in its entirety so you can get an overview of what can be done and where you are heading. After you read the entire section, I suggest you begin once again at the beginning of this section, using it as a guide for actual practice.

Ascension yoga is learning to attach ourselves to the Tree of Life that links all life systems in the universe to the Source of all Life. This is the art and science of raising the vibrational rate of the physical body to the point where we become "radiant light vehicles" that are worthy receptacles for our souls. When the soul and the body achieve the same energy state, the physical body is transformed. It is no longer fallen matter; it has been made sacred by achieving Christ Consciousness.

Attunement to Universal Love is the ultimate form of magic and shamanism. There is nothing more powerful. *The Keys of Enoch* makes it clear that Universal Love is the sustaining power and primary creative source of our universe. Therefore, when we consciously open ourselves up to the Universal Love of the Holy Spirit we access powers that enable us to transcend all lower-level illusions and distortions.

Ascension is breaking the spell of the Lord of the fallen light. Ascension is mastering the riddle of material existence. Ascension takes humanity beyond the third dimension, beyond this realm of fallen light and into the higher realms of fourth and fifth-dimensional existence and beyond.

Acceptance of the Universal Love of the Holy Spirit is the key teaching of the Master Christ. We need do nothing more than accept God's Love. It transcends all and heals all.

The Master Christ upset the controlling social priests of his day because he taught that all beings receive their sustenance from the Source, with no intermediaries needed. The primary illusion or distortion of our dimension is that we are somehow separate from God. The entities who want to keep us in darkness do not want us to know that we can easily access the Universal Love of the Holy Spirit by simply opening ourselves to receive it.

The ultimate form of mysticism is to become a clear channel for the Divine Light and Sacred Fire of God's Love. There is no higher form of magic and there is nothing more transformational or healing. Love is *the* Universal Energy.

GOD IS THE UNIVERSE,
THE UNIVERSE IS LOVE,
LOVE IS HARMONY.

CREATING THE TEMPLE

One of the most important basic concepts of working with the spiritual forces is that of creating a sacred space for our meditations and energy work with a meditation ceremony. This ceremony consists of claiming the space by cleansing and purifying it with Universal Love. This type of ceremony does not require elaborate preparation, only intention.

All schools of mysticism agree that spiritual progress is accelerated when it is done in a ceremonial manner. There are, of course, many types of spiritual ceremony, from the very elaborate to the very simple. What defines ceremony is the idea that the person or persons doing the ceremony have separated themselves from the mundane world by entering a space that has been set aside as a temple.

The temple can be a permanent construction such as a room or other space that is set aside for spiritual purposes, or it can be made by simply *visualizing a protective circle or Pillar of Light around oneself.* Claiming the space in this manner is an important spiritual practice, because this creates a clear separation from the mundane world.

It can be fun to create a beautiful space in which to do spiritual work, but it must be remembered that objects do not make the temple. The sacred space of the temple is created with *intention* and *spirit,* not architecture. Nonetheless, it should be noted that the classic circle-and-cross design which is used as the standard temple arrangement in both western magic and the Native American Medicine Wheel is symbolic of Universal Love and the High Pleiadian star energies. The circle and cross design acts as an antenna that brings in and resonates with Christ Consciousness energies.

CREATING ENERGY FIELDS AS AN ACT OF WILL

Creating energy fields is easier than many people realize. It is done by simply *Willing* the energy to manifest and then seeing it happen in the mind's eye. Energy flows where thought goes. To create an energy field around ourselves, we need to simply think about its happening and then reinforce that thought with a mental command for this thing to actually occur. Mental commands set the *Will* in motion; the *Will* then does what it can to manifest the reality of the thoughts: we are able to *think* energy fields into being and direct energy wherever we desire.

Will is the power of manifestation. The *Will* is directed by thought. To control the *Will,* one must be in control of the way one uses language, verbally and internally. Don Juan often spoke to Carlos Castaneda about the "control of internal dialogue" (language in the mind).

CREATING A SACRED SPACE WITH INTENTION:
THE EXORCISM OF NEGATIVE ENTITIES

Working with energy fields such as the Pillar of Light is an important aspect of ascension yoga. We create energy fields around ourselves to protect, heal, and energize our bodies, our temples, and our homes. The creation of energy fields is one of the first exercises students of yoga and mysticism learn. The Body of Light is activated and strengthened as you develop your ability to work with energy fields.

We can make any space a sacred space with our intention. All schools of mysticism I am familiar with recommend calling in the "Light" to bless and clear our homes and bodies of negative energies and entities.

One of the most important concepts of ceremony and temple work is to claim the space by filling it with your presence, and then demanding, out loud, in the name of the Lord God Creator of the universe that any and all negative entities that may be present leave and never return. As this is done, cleanse and purify the area by mentally creating a Pillar of Light that brings the Universal Love vibrations directly into The space – And ask out loud that this be done.

Our bodies, our homes, and our cars should also be blessed and purified in the manner described above. Blessing and exorcism are very important aspects of magic and shamanism. It is wise to use exorcism to make sure that no strange entities are lurking around your home, your temple, your associates, or yourself. **To avoid karmic penalties you must always ask permission to do any type of energy work or exorcism on anyone other than yourself.**

You will quite likely note a definite shift in energy around yourself and your home after you begin your blessings and exorcisms.

INVOCATION FOR EXORCISM OF NEGATIVE ENTITIES

I INVOKE THE HOLY SPIRIT
IN THE NAME OF THE LORD GOD CREATOR OF THE UNIVERSE.
I DEMAND THAT ANY AND ALL NEGATIVE ENTITIES
WHO MAY BE ATTACHED TO ME ON THE INNER PLANES
OR THAT ARE OTHERWISE ATTEMPTING TO
MANIPULATE ME IN ANY WAY
LEAVE ME NOW!
I CALL OUT TO MY HIGHER SELF
I CALL OUT TO MY SOUL
I CALL OUT TO MY ANGELIC GUIDES,
BE WITH ME! GUIDE ME! PROTECT ME!

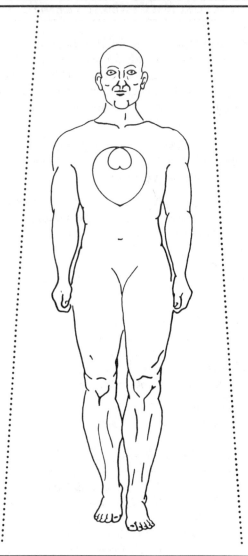

To succeed in the practice of ascension yoga, we must remember to remain well grounded. The Earth is our focal point in the universe; it is our spaceship. When we reaffirm our Earth connection, we complete the energy circuit from the higher realms into the physical, thus creating an energy conduit for the transformational energies of Spirit. The Hawaiian shamen, the Kahunas, teach that the unconscious mind is an aspect of the Earth itself, and it is only when the unconscious mind is in harmony with the planet that it will begin pulling in the high mana of the Higher Self. It is helpful to think of oneself as an energy circuit between the Higher Self and the Earth. The Pillar of Light is the **RAINBOW BRIDGE.**

THE PILLAR OF LIGHT – RAINBOW BRIDGE TO THE HIGHER SELF

The Pillar of Light and its central channel, the Antahkarana, are a two-way energy circuit, from the Earth to the eighth chakra Soul Star, and from the eighth chakra back to the Earth. To perform energy transformation of the physical body and to reprogram DNA we must use the breath, visualization, and the Pillar of Light/Antahkarana to draw Kundalini Life-Force Energy up from the Earth, and Solar Life Force Energy (Prana) down from the eighth chakra.

Earth energy flows naturally into the chakras in the base of our feet and through the area around the tip of the spine and the perineum. It is good to meditate directly on the land, using the chakras at the tip of your spine, perineum, and bottoms of your feet to send energetic roots deep into the Earth.

Grounding ourselves into the Earth is an important part of the ceremony of the Pillar of Light. *The Keys of Enoch* tells us that we must learn to heal the Earth by invoking Universal Love as the Holy Spirit and projecting it into the Earth. One of the ways to do this is to visualize yourself as part of an energy channel that extends to the very center of the Earth, and then use your *Will* to send Love into our planet's heart.

THE PILLAR OF LIGHT AS A CHANNEL FOR UNIVERSAL LOVE

The Keys of Enoch mentions the Pillar of Light many times, making it clear that this is one of the most powerful transformational and protective techniques we can use.

⊕   The Pillar of Light is an important basic exercise.
⊕   Its practice can be traced back at least as far as the ancient Egyptians.
⊕   When using the Pillar of Light, the student makes a direct connection with their Higher Self/Soul.
⊕   The Pillar of Light brings the student guidance from the entities who support the positive evolution of humanity.
⊕   The Pillar of Light energizes the student and brings the student's energy bodies into Harmony.
⊕   The Pillar of Light forms a protective shield around the student.
⊕   The Pillar of Light can be used to cleanse the aura of negativity and blockages.
⊕   The Pillar of Light should be invoked before meditating or before doing healing work.
⊕   The Pillar of Light should be used in conjunction with the various invocations and prayers given in this book.

AFTER THE PILLAR OF LIGHT IS INVOKED, IT SHOULD BE LEFT ON!

Stand with your feet spread about as far apart as the width of your head. Keep your knees slightly bent, as this allows energy to flow freely through the leg area. If the knees are locked, the muscle tension will block the energy flow. After you have found your point of balance visualize a Pillar of gold or white Light surrounding your body. See this Pillar of Light rising far above you and descending far below you into the Earth.

Use your powers of creative visualization and *Will* to draw Soul Star energy in through your crown chakra with your breath, then use your *Will* to circulate this energy throughout your body.

See Spirit, feel Spirit, breathe Spirit.

Use the invocations that are given in this book to program the energies of the Pillar of Light to cleanse, purify, and heal your body and mind.

I invoke my Soul.
Be with me,
Shield me, protect me.
Help me learn how to create the Pillar of Light.
Aloha

I Am Universal Harmony.
I Am Universal Balance.
I Am Universal Love.
I Am Universal Life.
I Am Universal Light.
I Am One with the Infinite Universe.
I Am all powerful.
I invoke the power of mental clarity.

EARTH HEALING AND PILLAR OF LIGHT EXERCISES

⊕ Use the Pillar of Light to send healing energy into the Earth.
⊕ Use the Pillar of Light to send healing Love into the Earth.
⊕ Use the Pillar of Light to send prayers into the Earth.
⊕ Use the Pillar of Light to send your consciousness into the Earth.

THE ANTAHKARANA AND THE PILLAR OF LIGHT

The Antahkarana originates in the realm of the Soul. It is the central channel within the Pillar of Light: the interdimensional link between the superconscious energies of the Higher Self/Soul Star and the physical body.

The Antahkarana enters the physical body at the crown chakra, passes through the center of the body, exits the body at the perineum, and terminates just below the feet, or in the Earth's core.

The Antahkarana is the etheric counterpart of the spinal column. But it is not inside the spinal column – it passes through the center of the body – in front of the spine.

The Antahkarana is the central axis of your physical body. All of your energy fields, including the Merkaba, spin around the Antahkarana.

USING THE PILLAR OF LIGHT AND ANTAHKARANA TO INVOKE THE HIGHER SELF AND THE SOUL

The fastest and most direct route to spiritual development is to access the Soul through the use of the Pillar of Light/Antahkarana, as detailed in this book.

The Soul has at least three distinct levels that are appropriate to discuss at this time: the Higher Self, the Christ Overself, and the Soul – the highest aspect of consciousness.
Higher Self is the lower aspect of the Soul, it is the intermediary level between Universal Consciousness and physicality. It is the first aspect of the Soul most students make contact with.

The difference between this type of work and standard yoga meditation is that instead of meditating for years to attune oneself to the Higher Self, the process is accelerated by activating the Pillar of Light/Antahkarana with the *Will*, and then using these energy channels to send prayers and energy directly to the Higher Self.

Ceremony, meditation, invocation, and visualization are important practices in the invocation of the Higher Self and the Soul. The student calls out to the Higher Self in meditation and prayer to let it know that its physical aspect desires to commence the great work.

When the Higher Self and Soul are contacted in this manner, the Pillar of Light/Antahkarana become an open channel for Soul Star energies that rapidly cleanse and purify the physical and mental bodies, removing all types of negative karma, energy blockages, possessions, curses, and spells.

The Pillar of Light and Antahkarana can by used as a channel to send prayers and invocations to the Universal Mind, via the Higher Self and Soul.

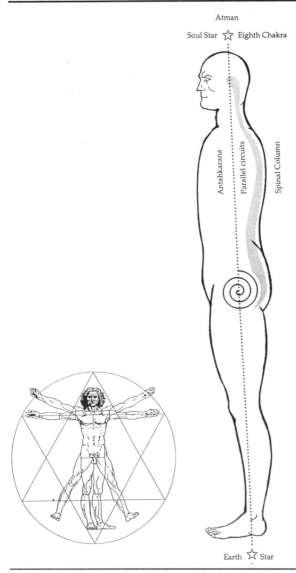

Atman

Soul Star ☆ Eighth Chakra

Antahkarana   Parallel circuits   Spinal Column

Earth ☆ Star

The Antahkarana is the center of the Pillar of Light.
We strengthen our connection with our Higher Self and our Soul
by meditating upon the reality of the Pillar of Light/Antahkarana.

The spine and the Antahkarana are parallel to one another. The Antahkarana is an etheric tube of Light that enters the body at the crown chakra and exits the body at the perineum. The Antahkarana is the axis for the spiraling energy field of the Merkaba. We strengthen the Merkaba by using the *Will* and the breath to draw energy down from the Soul Star and up from the Earth – then *Willing* these energies to expand out from the heart chakra into the auric field.

The goal of all these exercises is to attune the physical body to the energies of Soul, thus allowing the energies of Universal Consciousness to merge with the conscious mind and physical body. This process occurs in stages and is governed by the student's willingness to do the work required to bring this into fruition.

I Am that I Am,
I call out to my Soul, hear me:
Open the channel between us,
Activate the Pillar of Light,
cleanse this unit,
purify this unit,
heal this unit,
I open myself to receive
The blessings of the Infinite Spirit
In all things.

I ask the Holy Spirit to place a Pillar of its Divine Essence over me.
I ask the Great Spirit for help, guidance, and protection.
I invoke the presence of my Soul.
Be with me, help me, guide me, protect me.
Show me the path to ascension
and everlasting life in ever-expanding life systems.

I Am that I Am,
I cancel, nullify, and dissolve any and all
negative and undesirable energies or karma
I may have accumulated in this lifetime
Or any other lifetime
And I now activate and accept
the Christ Consciousness program
within every cell of my being

INVOCATION OF THE SOUL FOR EXORCISM

I invoke the presence of my Soul.
I *Will* my Soul to remove all entities
that may be attached to any of my bodies.
I *Will* my Soul to cancel, nullify, and dissolve
any and all curses and hexes
that have ever been directed toward me,
or that affect me in any way.

AS HUMAN BEINGS WE ARE NATURALLY TELEPATHIC

It is generally accepted among the schools of mystic thought that the primary reason the average person is not aware of the psychic energy they are constantly broadcasting and receiving is that their conscious mind filters out these signals. Many reasons may be given for this filtering, but the most obvious cause of this is that most people are trained from childhood to ignore psychic energy and concentrate on the sensory input of the physical sensory organs.

Telepathy is prayer! When we focus our thoughts on Divinity and send out thoughts in the form of prayers we are practicing telepathy and communicating with the Universal Mind of God and our Soul. Students on the path who are a bit more advanced than the common Sunday School student may also work on sending telepathic messages (prayers) to Angels, extraterrestrial groups, and inner-plane masters.

Humans naturally send and receive psychic energy transmissions; therefore, it is quite easy to establish telepathic contact with Angelic entities. All one needs to do is:

⊕   To go into a quiet meditative state.
⊕   Invoke the Pillar of Light.
⊕   Use the power of *Will* to clear the space of undesirable energies.
⊕   Make a prayer to qualify the energy.
⊕   Use the power of the *Will* and creative imagination to send out mental requests for contact.
⊕   Open the mind to receive replies.

As you develop your psychic abilities, you will discover that your body is an antenna for various types of spiritual energies, and that at all times your body is sampling and reacting to the vibrations that surround it. Your heart will know many things before your mind gets its first clue. You will find in particular that you will be able to sense the physical presence and temperament of other humans with your body. This is known as listening with the heart.

UNCONSCIOUS TELEPATHY

Be aware of the fact that our bodies are energy beacons that attract various forms of nonphysical life. When a human is filled with love and joy, positive entities are attracted into their spiritual circle. On the other hand, if a human becomes immersed in negative thought forms, their aura becomes a beacon that may attract negative discarnates who feed on the energy that negative emotions produce.

Since ancient times, humans who desire spiritual advancement have called on Angels for help, guidance, and protection.

The ceremonial invocation of the Angels is an important part of ascension yoga. It is quite traditional for mystics to call upon Angels to help them in their quest for knowledge and/or power. The Angels are our guides and helpers. One of their missions is to assist evolving beings in their quest for initiation into increasingly higher dimensional realities.

We are advised, however, that Angels obey the Law of Free Will. Because of this, they do not usually interfere with the lives of individual humans unless they are asked to do so. Once the Angels are formally invited to actively participate in one's life, they become a powerful force with seemingly unlimited capabilities to help, guide, and protect.

The invocation of an Angel is not difficult, as each human has an Angel awaiting their call (the Guardian Angel). Invoking this Angel establishes a dialogue between the conscious mind and the Angel. If done properly, this invocation also gives the Angel permission to help the student.

Besides the very important task of offering humanity protection against negative forces, the Angels also act as guides to inner-plane work, holding the keys to many doors. As you develop your practice of ascension yoga, you will want to ask your Angelic guide to help you learn how to access the transformational energies of Spirit as well as the knowledge of the inner planes.

It is important to mention that a technical system of Angel entities known as Enochian Magic has been with us in its present form since the mid-1500s. It is my opinion that this particular form of spiritual exploration could be unhealthy to the practitioner. I advise all of you who wish to work with Angels to be very aware of which type of Angel or extraterrestrial you call in. The safest test seems to be to qualify all of your invocations with a clause that identifies them with the Lord God of Hosts, such as the following:

"I ask for an Angel in service to the
Lord God of Hosts to come to me."

In the ceremony for the invocation of an Angel, the words Great Spirit, Creator of All Things, and Lord of the Universe qualify the energy of the prayer as being in alignment with the celestial hierarchy that works for the positive evolution of humanity, as does the mantra Kodoish, Kodoish, Kodoish, Adonai 'Tsebayoth.

The more serious you are about this work, the more real the work becomes. This does not mean that one must be stern; it simply means that ceremonies done in a properly prepared space and spoken in a strong voice will be more effective.

Oh Great Spirit, Creator of all things, Lord of the Universe,
please hear my prayer.
I thank you for my life and the gift of consciousness.
I thank you for all the things you have given me.
I ask for help, guidance, and protection.
I ask that I be guided on the path of ascension.
I ask to have my psychic abilities awakened.

Oh Great Spirit, Creator of all things, Lord of the Universe,
I ask that you assign an Angelic Master of Light to me
to help me learn the high science of divine attunement.

After the Angel has been invoked, you may ask it to help you.

In the name of the Great Spirit, Creator of all things, Lord of the Universe,
I thank you, my Angel, for being here to help me.
In the name of the Great Spirit, Creator of all things, Lord of the Universe,
I ask that you, my Angelic guide, help me, guide me, and protect me.
I ask that you help me activate the energy circuits
That control my ability to work with the Spiritual Lights.
I ask that you begin helping me in these things now.

Oh Great Spirit, Creator of all things, Lord of the Universe,
I ask that you make your Light known to me,
so that I will be able to fulfill my life's mission
and honor you in all things that I do.
Oh Great Spirit, Creator of all things, Lord of the Universe,
I ask that your help, guidance, and protection be with me
throughout all time, all space, and all realities.

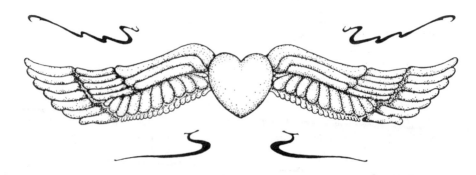

EXERCISE ONE

1. Use a black background such as a piece of cardboard.
2. Use a light that has a dimmer.
3. Hold your hand 1/2 " over cardboard and dim the light until it cannot be seen.
4. After a while, your eyes will adjust and the your hand will become visible.
5. Focus on one area of your hand. Within 11 seconds a blue-white aura should become visible between your fingers.

EXERCISE TWO

1. Use a white square of cardboard about 24" on a side.
2. Obtain several bright squares of cardboard about 8" across.
3. Using a bright light, gaze at one of the colored squares as you hold it in front of the white board. Do this for about one minute.
4. When the colored square is removed, an afterimage of the square's complementary color will appear in your field of vision.
5. Gaze at this color image until it fades. This will train the brain to understand how to see colors that are not directly associated with physical objects.

EXERCISE THREE – SEEING HUMAN AURAS

1. This exercise requires that a human subject dresses in white.
2. A white background and a bright light are required.
3. Hold the colored squares of cardboard in front of the subject.
4. When the colored square is removed an afterimage of the square's complementary color will appear.
5. Gaze at this color image until it fades. This will train the brain to understand how to see colors that are not directly associated with physical objects.
6. In a short period of time the average student will begin to see genuine auric colors around the subject. Once this occurs the student will find that the auric colors will change as the thoughts of the subject change. The colors around the head will generally reflect the thoughts, while the colors around the body will generally reflect the emotions.

Please take note of the fact that sight takes place in the **mind** not in the eyes! The eyes are merely energy receptors, and they are limited to a very narrow bandwidth in the physical electromagnetic spectrum. The mind itself, however, is without limit of vision. We must therefore realize that in order to see auras our focus of perception needs to be shifted from the physical eyes, to the inner eye of the mind itself. So relax, and simply allow yourself to experience what comes naturally.

By learning the body's basic energy circuits and a few basic breath and visualization exercises, we gain the tools to effectively begin transforming the physical body into a Body of Light.

The art and practice of working with life force energy is a life-long study that can be interpreted in many ways. In the following pages we will explore some of the basic ideas about the human energy system that are common to all schools, as well as a few concepts that are "esoteric."

One of the most important aspects of this art that a beginner must understand is that the spinal column is the primary energy channel of the physical body. (Just as the Antahkarana is the primary energy channel of the Light Body.) life-force energy flows between the chakras via the spinal column. The most profound experience a human can have while still in the physical body is to energize the spine to the point of life-force superconductivity, otherwise known as the Kundalini experience. To evolve spiritually we must continuously work on strengthening the flow of life force energy in the spinal column. This is done with breath, visualization, and "locks" (bandhas).

It is easy to learn how to work with spiritual energy, and developing skill in this art can quite fairly be compared to physical exercise and conditioning. If one does not exercise, they will have weak muscles. If a person with weak muscles exercises, they will develop strength. It is not surprising that many people claim that they cannot feel energy. They have never been taught how to do it, and they have never exercised their spiritual muscles. I find it quite rewarding to work with beginners because their first experiences with universal life force energies are always quite a revelation.

Soon after the beginning student starts practicing running energy circuits through the spine and the Antahkarana, the body's entire etheric energy system becomes activated and strengthened.

In the west we usually speak of the seven-chakra system. We must understand that within the physical body there are numerous chakras beside the seven major chakras, including three that are as important as the seven most books mention: the rear heart chakra (between the shoulderblades); the "mouth of God," or medulla oblongata (at the base of the brain, in back of the head); and the Bindu (behind the crown chakra at the top of the head).

It is interesting to note that some Tibetan schools group the three chakras in the abdomen together and refer to them as the **"Lower Cauldron,"** the place where life force energy is stored, processed and "cooked." The understanding of the processing of energy in the lower three chakras is important in the practice of transformational yoga and healing, as the chakras of the Lower Cauldron can be utilized to store, amplify and project energy throughout the body and beyond.

These basic ideas can be used as a foundation for developing your own meditations. As you progress, you will receive advanced instructions from your Higher Self, an Angelic guide, or directly from the Universal Mind.

THE BREATH

To develop awareness of the body's energy circuits, practice using the *Will* and creative visualization to breathe energy through the chakras and the spine. The control of the breath is essential to yoga and healing. In the eastern Indian schools of yoga, the art and science of breathing is known by the Sanskrit word pranayama, which means "control of the life force," or "expansion of life force." In the human body, life force automatically circulates with the breath. We can control and modify the flow of life force through the body by becoming aware of how energy follows the breath.

There are four stages of breathing: inhalation, retention, exhalation, and the pause. During inhalation and exhalation, we follow the energy circuits of the body, thus awakening them. During retention, we process and integrate life-force energy. When exhaling we can use this natural outflowing of life force energy to increase the amount of energy we project from our heart chakra or our hands.

USING THE ROOT LOCK TO CONTROL LIFE FORCE ENERGY

One of the ways that yogis have found to process, integrate, and project life force is to use locks. There are three primary locks: the throat, the solar plexus, and the root. We will discuss the root lock only, because it has the ability to increase our power and our ability to project energy, and because it has been kept secret for ages.

The root lock increases our ability to absorb, hold and project life force energy. The root is the base chakra. Primal life force energy (Shakti Kundalini) is known to enter the root chakra at the base of the spine and leave the root chakra through the area of the perineum.

To perform this lock, *slightly* tighten the muscles in the area of the perineum as the breath is drawn in. This closes the area of the base chakra where life-force energy is known to leave the body. Applying this lock causes extra energy to build up in the Lower Cauldron. The key to this lock is remembering that as the breath is drawn in, the perineum should be tightened a little. When the breath is released, the perineum should become relaxed. Tightening the perineum too much will cause discomfort, so be sure to listen to your body.

Working with the breath and the power of creative visualization stimulates energy flow in the spine, the chakras, and the various etheric energy channels.

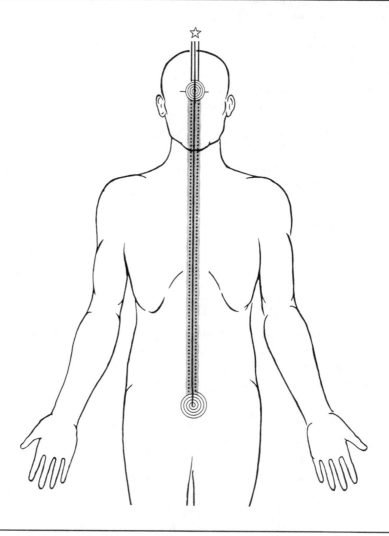

There are three channels for life-force energy in the spine: the central nerve channel and two hollow channels that run parallel to it. The right channel *Pingala*, carries Prana – solar masculine life-force energy. The left channel *Ida*, carries Shakti Kundalini – feminine life-force energy. The central nerve channel, *Shushumna*, is where these two energies intertwine to create the state of superconductivity known as enlightenment. The central nerve channel should not be confused with the Antahkarana, which is also referred to as the central channel. The Antahkarana is an etheric tube of light that goes through the center of the body from the crown chakra to the perineum; it is not in the spine.

ALWAYS breathe through the nose unless doing an exercise that requires you to breathe through the mouth.

ALWAYS keep tongue at the roof of the mouth to complete the circuit.

INHALE, using your *Will* to draw spiritual energy in through the crown chakra, down the spine to the Lower Cauldron (chakras 1,2,3). As you draw in the breath, you apply the root lock.

HOLD the breath and the root lock for a moment, as you allow the energy in the Lower Cauldron to build up.

RELEASE the breath and the root lock and use the *Will* to send the energy up the spine from the Lower Cauldron to the crown chakra and third eye, thus activating these chakras and awakening dormant brain cells.

Soul Star ∞ Eighth Chakra

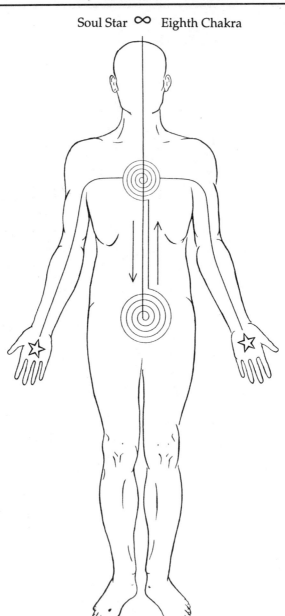

With the breath, spiritual energy is brought in through the crown chakra and down the spine to the Lower Cauldron. It is held there for a few moments and allowed to build up. When this energy is released, the *Will* is used to direct the energy up the spine to the heart chakra and then out through the arms to the hands.

It is suggested that each meditation session begin with an invocation. The following two invocations use word symbolism that works both on the conscious and unconscious minds to produce a relaxed state that is receptive to higher knowledge.

When reading the following statements you will see that they contain a series of clauses that address the various aspects or levels of the mind – physical, spiritual and universal. Please notice how these statements move through various layers of consciousness creation.

It is also suggested that the student tape-record these statements and play them during their meditations until they feel ready to create their own. It is a good idea to actually memorize an invocation that you repeat at the beginning of the meditation ceremony.

VERSION ONE

I Am That I Am.
I *Will* myself to be as calm and receptive as the Universal Waters.
I open myself to receive the Light of Universal Truth.
I Am one with all that is; the Kingdom of God is within.
I Am the inner, I Am the outer,
I Am the higher, I Am the lower,
I Am without limit, I Am that I Am
Throughout all time, all space and all dimensional realities.
I Am a perfect jewel that reflects the Universal Light of Truth.

VERSION TWO

Peace, peace, peace,
I calm the infinite waters of my mind.
I invoke the Universal Light of Truth.
I Am one with all that is;
the Kingdom of God is within
I Am the inner, I Am the outer,
I Am the higher, I Am the lower.
I Am without limit.
I Am awareness within awareness,
I Am consciousness within consciousness.
I Am That I Am,
Throughout all time, all space and all dimensional realities.
I Am a perfect jewel that reflects the Universal Light of Truth.

Many spiritual traditions recommend that students practice merging their consciousness with the universe. When we achieve harmony with the universe, the gifts of Spirit flow freely to us.

Regularly visualizing oneself as being part of the universe is a very powerful exercise that puts us in direct contact with the primal forces of creation. When we access universal consciousness, we transcend the distortions of the physical plane and receive protection, power, and inspiration directly from the Source.

Students of mysticism gain many spiritual gifts by reaffirming their connection with the universe through meditation and by regularly thinking of themselves as being one with the universe, seeing no separation between the self and the All.

The student must let go of the illusion of somehow being separate from the universe. To see oneself as being separate from the universe is to see oneself as being separate from God. To be separate from God is impossible.

The universe is infinite. To attune oneself with the universe places one in harmony with powers that have no limit. True schools of mystery have always known this, yet it has remained somewhat of a secret to the outer world.

UNIVERSAL ATTUNEMENT MEDITATION

1. Invoke the Pillar of Light. See the room filled with Golden Light.
2. Demand that all negatives leave your space.
3. Pray to the Great Spirit, asking for guidance and protection.
4. Mentally repeat the mantra below.

As you repeat the mantra given below, visualize the star fields of infinite space. See yourself among these stars. See the stars as your body. See the stars as points of Light on your acupuncture meridians. See these points of Light being anchored in your body.

I AM UNIVERSAL HARMONY
I AM ONE WITH THE INFINITE STAR FIELDS OF DIVINE CREATION

I AM UNIVERSAL HARMONY
I AM ONE WITH THE INFINITE STAR FIELDS OF DIVINE CREATION

I AM UNIVERSAL HARMONY
I AM ONE WITH THE INFINITE STAR FIELDS OF DIVINE CREATION

BECOMING A CLEAR CHANNEL FOR THE PERFECT LIGHT
OF INFINITE WISDOM

In order to become a clear channel for the Light we must clear out any negative mental complexes that we may have taken on during the course of our lives. Negative mental complexes create energy blockages and distortions that prevent the highly refined energies of Spirit from flowing freely through the various energy channels of the physical and etheric bodies each one of us possesses.

The most common and often the most effective techniques for the removal or dissolution of negative mental complexes use language structure modification. Most students are, of course, familiar with the basic form of language structure modification, which is commonly referred to as *positive thought*.

Beyond simply using positive thought and engaging in positive action, the student is encouraged to engage in self-analysis and the exploration of their own psyche in order that they better understand what the underlying factors that motivate them to think or behave as they do.

The most common negative mental complexes are fear, guilt, and the belief in sin. It is also known that these three concepts frequently act in synergy and validate one another. (Hate, anger, lust, envy, resentment, and emotional trauma are also recognized as the basis for many common negative mental complexes.)

Concepts such as sin, guilt and fear are known to be limiting and constricting thoughtforms. When these concepts are accepted into the workings of a mind as reality, they cause that mind to become closed to the pure Light of Truth that emanates from the Infinite Universal Mind, the I Am Presence. These thought forms are what we could describe as lower dimensional thought or limited thought.

The Universal Mind knows no limits. This is known and understood by all schools of advanced spiritual or metaphysical thought. The Universal Mind does not program its creation to be sinful or guilty, and it does not expect its creations to live in fear of the Great Central Sun. The Universal Mind is Light, Life, Love.

The ultimate substance of the universe is Love: Universal Love. Anything that does not reflect the Love of the Supreme Creator is a *distortion*. Sin, guilt, and fear are distortions of the pure Love emanations of Godhead. These distortions exist only in lower-dimensional universes such as our own.

Aligning ourselves with the infinite Light of Love is even more powerful than language structure modification and positive thought, as Universal Love transmutes all forms of negativity and distortion on all levels of existence, from etheric to subatomic. *All of the techniques in this book that involve working with the Pillar of Light, the Antahkarana, and the Merkaba bring in Universal Life-Force Energies that transmute distortions and blockages in the various bodies of the human vehicle (pranic psychotherapy).*

Begin by calming yourself, grounding yourself and by invoking the Pillar of Light. Use the energy of your Higher Self - Soul Star to empower your words and bring them into manifestation.

I Am That I Am; I cancel, nullify and dissolve all vows or agreements that I have made in this or any other life that keep me from accessing the Light of Universal Truth.

I Am That I Am; I cancel and nullify all vows or agreements that I may have made with any and all entities that may be attempting to keep me from accessing the Light of Universal Truth.

I Am That I Am; I release any and all entities that may be attempting to keep me from accessing the Light of Universal Truth.

I Am That I Am; I dissolve any bonds or connections that I may have to any and all entities that may be attempting to keep me from accessing the Light of Universal Truth.

I Am That I Am; I de-curse myself, I de-hex myself, I de-haunt myself.

In the name of the I Am That I Am, I ask that the Master Jesus Christ or one of his Angelic helpers bind all entities that may have been released from me and take them to the regions of pure Love. And so it is, now.

In the name of The I Am That I Am, I command and I do demand in the name of the Holy Spirit that any and all entities that may be attempting to control me or use my energy in any way leave me now and do not return. And I demand that they do not attach themselves to any other sentient being. And that if any entities have been present here or attached to me in any way, I ask that the Master Christ or one of his servants guide these entities to the regions of pure Love and that they manipulate no sentient being ever again. In the name of the most high and Holy Spirit I demand this and make it so now.

TRUTH IS THE LIGHT THAT SHINES FORTH FROM THE MIND OF GOD

TRUTH IS THE LIGHT THAT SHINES FORTH FROM THE MIND OF GOD

TRUTH IS THE LIGHT THAT SHINES FORTH FROM THE MIND OF GOD

I Am Universal Harmony.
I Am Universal Balance.
I Am Universal Love.
I Am Universal Life.
I Am Universal Light.
I Am One with the Infinite Universe.

METAPHYSICAL HEALING INVOCATIONS USING LOVE AND LIGHT TO ERASE DISTORTIONS AND ALIGN THE CONSCIOUSNESS VEHICLES WITH THE INFINITE LIGHT OF TRUTH THAT HEALS AND EMPOWERS ALL THINGS WITH LOVE

It is for my highest good to dissolve all blockages and distortions that keep me from accessing the Light of Universal Truth.

It is to my highest good to release all sin, guilt and fear.

I invoke the Light of Love; cleanse me.

I invoke the Light of Truth; inform me.

I invoke the Infinite Light; make me strong.

I Am That I Am,
I heal all things that have caused me pain,
I heal all wounds that I have received in this life or any other.

I invoke the Light of Life, Love and Truth; purify me.
In Universal Harmony and Balance, cleanse and heal all of my bodies.

I Am That I am, I cancel, nullify and
dissolve all negative mental complexes.

I Am That I Am, I cancel, nullify, and dissolve sin, guilt, and fear.

I forgive those who have hurt me or wronged me in any way,
and I ask that all those who have hurt me or wronged me,
to forgive me for creating the circumstances that led to our conflict.

I give thanks to the Universe for all blessings I have received
and all blessings I am to receive.

I ask for, and I do now invoke, the healing power of the Universal healing.

I Am the greatest healing power: I invoke the god within.

It is for my greatest good that I invite the presence of the
Holy Spirit into my being.

It is for my greatest good that I align my conscious mind with the
wisdom of my Soul.

51

DIAMOND MIND POWER FOR THE MERKABA MEDITATION

Visualize your Merkaba field as a diamond-crystal light lattice spinning around your body clockwise. With your thoughts, program this energy field so that each facet of the crystal is a magnetic mirror that both reflects and absorbs all things that are desirable and repels all things negative or undesirable.

I Am immortal and indestructible.
My mind is a diamond with a thousand faces.
I Am the luminous Body, I Am the jewel vehicle, I Am without limit.
My mind is a brilliant multifaceted diamond.
I Am a magnetic mirror that reflects the Light of Truth.
I Am that I Am.

I Am blessed by the Infinite Spirit in all things.
I Am immortal and indestructible.
My mind is a brilliant diamond with infinite facets.
I Am the luminous body, I Am the jewel vehicle, I Am without limit.
I Am the Merkaba Body of Light.
I activate my Merkaba field and open myself to receive advanced Light codes.

I AM BLESSED BY THE INFINITE SPIRIT IN ALL THINGS

I AM BLESSED BY THE INFINITE SPIRIT IN ALL THINGS

I AM BLESSED BY THE INFINITE SPIRIT IN ALL THINGS

The universal energies of Light, Life, and Love create a truth that is totally healing and empowering. The energies of Light, Life, and Love can be easily invoked to cancel, nullify, and dissolve all lower mental distortions such as fear, guilt, sin, anger, resentment, and any other thing that creates a veil, blockage, or distortion that resists the Light of the Ultimate Truth, which is God's Love.

Truth is the Light of God's infinite Mind. There is no truth but the Truth. When we live in Truth we reflect the Light of the Infinite Creator and the highest reality.

Truth is Light,
Light is Love,
Love is the highest good,
I ask the Light of Love to purify me,
I ask the Light of Love to heal me,
I ask the Light of Love to cleanse me,
I cancel, nullify, and dissolve all
blockages and distortions that
keep me from seeing the Inner Light.

HEAR ME MIND WITHIN MY MIND

I am the conscious entity that I call myself, I Am That I Am. The time is now come for my conscious mind to talk directly to my inner mind. It is now time for us to consciously begin working together to seek the Light of Truth. It is now time for us to affirm our friendship and our love for ourself. For in fact, we are the same being, and we share the same goal. I love you, I love myself, I am Universal Harmony, I am Universal Love, I am Universal Light, I invoke the Universal Light of Truth. Illuminate me.

I want to heal myself physically and spiritually, and thereby bring myself into harmony and alignment with the Infinite source of Creation and the creator of my soul. In my heart of hearts I know that there is no higher or more worthy goal.

Peace and harmony are the natural modes of human existence. It is time to heal myself by canceling, nullifying, and dissolving all negative mental complexes that have caused me to create realities that are neither peaceful, harmonious or life-enhancing.

It is to my highest good to cancel, nullify, and dissolve all guilt, fear and feelings of sinfulness or unworthiness. These concepts are artificial concepts and distortions that have no basis in the reality of the highest Universal Truths.

The Universal Mind does not recognize or deal in the concepts of guilt, sin, or fear. These concepts are self-created distortions of limited third-dimensional thought. There is no reason why I should allow myself to be affected by these limiting distortions. It is unnatural, undesirable, and unhealthy.

In the highest Truth the concepts known as sin, guilt and fear do not exist. In fact, the highest Truth is an aspect of Universal Light and Love. All Life is created and protected by Universal Light, Love and, Truth. This is the divine grace of the Holy Spirit. As I release the distortions of the third dimensional plane I will find great pleasure in the Truth of Truth.

The Light of Universal Love automatically cancels, nullifies, and dissolves all negative and undesirable mental complexes, as it cleanses, purifies, heals, and energizes my Diamond Body of Light.

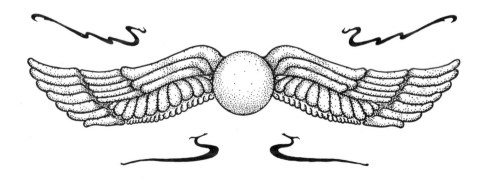

Please take note of these key phrases. Many of these words convey more than one level of meaning to the conscious and subconscious minds. It is a good idea to familiarize yourself with the various clauses contained in the statements below so that you have a stock of ideas to drawn on.

KEY WORDS

Love, Light, Life, Truth, Good, Heart, Jewel, Mind, Soul

I Am, Universal, Harmony, Balance, Now, Invoke, Thanks

KEY PHRASES

The Kingdom of God is within me.
I Am talking to my inner self .
I Am talking to the mind within my mind.
I Am That I Am.
I Am the inner, I Am the outer.
I Am all that there is.
I Am limitless.
I Am Universal Harmony.
I seek to know the highest Truth.
I seek to know the highest good.
I invoke the Light of Truth.
I invoke the Light of Love.
I seek Illumination.
I am soul manifest in the Earth.
I understand who I am.
Truth is Light.
Light is Love.

Most schools of magic, mysticism, and shamanism share a common belief in three primary levels of consciousness:

> The superconscious mind, or Higher Self.
> The conscious mind, or middle self.
> The unconscious mind, or lower self.

The superconscious mind is an aspect of Universal Consciousness and the Monad, it is the "inspirational body." The Soul, the Christ Overself, and the Higher Self are aspects of the superconscious mind.

The conscious mind is the middle self. It is the self-reflective analytical mind, or ego. The conscious mind has less information processing abilities than either the superconscious mind or the unconscious mind. The subconscious mind is an aspect of the middle self. The subconscious mind should not be confused with the unconscious mind, which is known to exist at a much deeper level.

The lower self is the unconscious mind. It should be understood, however, that the lower self is anything but unconscious. Compared to the conscious mind, the lower self is superconscious, as it automatically processes a great deal of energy and information. The first three chakras constitute the spiritual consciousness of the lower self: *Will*, manifestation, and the connection to primal, creative life force *Kundalini*. What psychologists refer to as the subconscious mind is the intermediary level between the conscious and unconscious minds.

Establishment psychologists echo the belief of the metaphysical schools in realizing that the unconscious mind processes much more information than the conscious mind, and that the *programs* of the unconscious mind are the underlying factors of behavior and personality. Metaphysical schools take this concept further, understanding that the unconscious mind also plays an important role in our ability to access spiritual gifts, because it controls *Will* and manifestation.

The unconscious mind can be compared to a computer because it runs our programs. We create our reality with the programs we have stored in our unconscious minds. These programs become both our personality and the interior structure of our mind. They are our *silent partner* who always has a say in what we think, do, or manifest, whether we realize it or not. It is therefore very important for us to realize that this is happening and to begin working on strengthening the link between our conscious and our unconscious minds.

Psychologists and mystics have observed that speech patterns are a reflection of the programs in the unconscious. It has also been determined that by using language in certain specific ways we can change the programming of the unconscious. This is the primary principle behind the use of mantras, invocation, hypnosis, and neurolinguistic programming. *Language is the structure of reality.*

We must clean up our thoughts in order to free ourselves from the bondage of negative thought patterns and the energies that go with those patterns. Overriding negative and undesirable thoughtforms begins by first taking charge of your thoughts, noticing how you feel about things, and then analyzing your thoughts to see which ones are positive and which ones are negative. The next step is consciously working on refining your thoughts and speech so that you do not create or empower negative sin, guilt, or fear programs.

When studying metaphysics or ascension yoga it is helpful to think of negative mental complexes such as guilt, sin, and fear as distortions that block the flow of nerve impulses and spiritual energy in the physical and etheric bodies.

In considering this subject it is important to take into account that each human is a multidimensional being. Therefore, it must also be understood that negative mental complexes are themselves multidimensional. They can exist within any part of the physical body, including the nervous system, the muscles, the bones, and organs. Negative mental complexes are karmic, therefore they also affect the causal body (otherwise known as the emotional body or karmic body).

Many of the concepts I employ come from Lama Anagarika's *Foundations of Tibetan Mysticism*. If some of the concepts given here do not agree with the terminology you are used to using, please remember that the various schools of mystic thought *do not have a consensus on terminology*. This creates a language problem and apparent contradictions. Therefore, what you may have been taught, or what you learn in the future may disagree somewhat with what is said here.

Inspirational Body – The Atman, Soul, Christ Overself, Higher Self. The Inspirational Body is an aspect of universal consciousness. (The Tibetans refer to this as the "the body of inspirational bliss.")

Manas – The Manas is the intuitive mind. It is the intermediary level between universal consciousness and the mental body. Manas participates in superconscious, conscious, and subconscious mental realities. It is an aspect of the Higher Self. *Mana*, as life-force energy, is equated with the infinite waters of space.

In the process of ascension and enlightenment the Manas is converted to the pure essence of awareness *Mani*, the "jewel vehicle" of perfected consciousness, *the true Luminous Body of the Merkaba*. The word "man" as a descriptive term for human beings is derived from the word Manas; therefore, it should be understood that in its original sense "man" is not a gender specific term. In its purest sense "man" denotes a being who thinks.

Consciousness Body – Totality of activities beyond active thought. Interpenetrated by the causal body.

Thought Body or Mental Body – Personality or ego. (Ego is the concept of separateness from the universe – *individuality*.) The thought body is interpenetrated by the causal body. The "lower mind" of the thought body is exclusively involved with dialogue.

Causal Body – The *karma body*. While the word "causal" may be somewhat of an awkward phrase, it is nonetheless descriptive of the underlying *cause* behind our earthly conditions. The causal body carries the energy patterns that create the circumstances of physical existence – karma. Some of the patterns in the causal body may be carried over from previous incarnations. The Causal Body is sometimes referred to as the emotional body.

The Mind – The vehicle and tool of the soul. Mind, like the physical body, is a *shell* created by the soul to explore the lower world of physical creation.

Pranic Body – Also called astral body, light body, etheric body, and subtle body. The pranic body is sustained by the breath. The Pranic Body is not the Light Body of the Merkaba, but the Merkaba is powered with Prana.

Physical Body – The primal Earth-bound consciousness vehicle.

Many schools of philosophical thought agree that ours is a free will universe and that we have the power to do as we will, but we must remember that free will can be abused. The *fall* of Adam and Eve is an interesting example of this. Eve was not forced to eat the apple, she was *tricked* into doing it.

In a free will universe, entities are free to abuse other entities. Yes, there may be a karmic penalty involved, but not all entities believe in karma.

Free will can be manipulated. A human can be made to choose misery by their own free will! An example of this is that many people choose to smoke, and it ultimately may make them miserable. Yet no one forces them to do it; they choose to smoke of their own free will. There are many other examples; just look around.

Free will under the Law of Love will never hurt another.

Free will can be manipulated in ways that cause us to unwittingly do things that are not good for us as individuals, or as a society.

Negative entities that operate on the astral plane feed on human fear. These entities have worked long and hard to trick us into arranging our world in such a manner that many humans become locked into a cycle of fear.

Breaking this cycle is both easy and difficult. It is easy because all that is required is to allow ourselves to become full of love and joy. It is difficult because society conditions people to focus on life's negative and undesirable aspects.

Can you override years of negative thought and action? Hopefully, the answer is yes. If you were so far gone that you could not feel joy and love, you would not be reading this book. Practice feeling happy about things. Instead of looking at negative aspects of situations, find the positive aspects. Work on this a little at a time, bringing in more love and letting go of more negativity. The more love and joy you experience, the more harmony you will find in your life. Love, joy, and harmony empower one another. When you find harmony the universe sends you increased amounts of love, and love creates Joy. When you are in a harmonious state, you are immune to the negative entities and their programming. A powerful exercise for overriding negative programs is to simply meditate on loving yourself.

Love is the ultimate creative force in the universe. Love is strength, not weakness or vulnerability. Remember that the Master Christ taught love as a solution to all things. But also remember that you have the free will to say "no" to established social and religious institutions that teach fear and intolerance.

The negative forces prefer that Earth humans do not believe in the spiritual realms or in the entities that occupy them.

As long as an enemy is invisible it is invincible.

White magicians know that great things can be accomplished by aligning themselves with the Angels that support positive human evolution, who are in the service of the Lord God. They also know that great harm can be done by consorting with the fallen ones. Unfortunately, due to the way our society has been structured, it is far easier for the average human to find himself consorting with fallen entities than with entities of the Light.

All schools of magic and mysticism that I am familiar with teach that there are planes of existence that parallel our own, and that the acceptance of the reality of the existence of these inner planes or spiritual dimensions is of primary importance to the understanding of the nature of existence.

Angels, demons, elementals, and various types of discarnate evolutionary beings exist on dimensional realities that somehow overlap or parallel our physical dimension. It is particularly important to be aware that some negative entities feed on the psychic energy discharge of the human aura. On a regular basis these entities attach themselves to unsuspecting humans and suck their energy. And unless the host human complains and makes some effort to free himself from this type of possession, he is at the mercy of these vampires.

Much human suffering is caused by these vampires and their allies. They have found that humans who are out of balance with fear or hate are easier to feed off of than humans who are in balance. These entities also know that they can manipulate the Law of Free Will to their advantage. They know they do not have to ask permission to commit acts of vampirism on unsuspecting humans. Free will is often abused. These entities know that as long as their host does not complain and command them to leave, they can do as they please.

Mystery schools emphasize that we must take measures to protect ourselves from negative, inner-plane entities. Often, the first thing students are taught to do is to shield themselves by visualizing themselves surrounded with white or golden Light and *Willing* it to be so. The next phase is what is known as exorcism, which is the practice of driving away negative spirits.

One thing that is particularly ironic about possession is the fact that many humans do not accept the existence of the inner planes. Even among those who do, there are few who have claimed their power and demanded that the negative spirits leave them alone. I suggest you ceremonially exorcise yourself and your home regularly, and then remember to ask the Angels of Light to enter.

In the name of the Lord God Creator of all things, I demand that any and all negative entities that may be attached to me in any way or who are using my energy in any way stop now and leave me forever, now! I command this; leave me now! Leave my home and my car now! Leave! and bother no one again!

True mystics carefully choose their words to reflect the reality they want to create. They know that the words we use reinforce our reality and that it is important to use positive language that does not limit us or curse us. Each one of us needs to look at the way we use language and realize that the words we use in our daily lives should be as carefully chosen as the words we use in our prayers, mantras, and invocations.

The Keys of Enoch refers to English as a "secondary language." This means our language has lost its resonance with the perfect universal waveforms of God consciousness. The vibrations of the words do not reflect the image of the words. This is yet another way we have been robbed of our connection with universal consciousness: we have been given a language that has little power.

Referring to English as a secondary language also indicates that our language has been constructed in a way that causes us to create limited and distorted realities. Even so, we still create our reality with this fallen language – a sobering thought.

Our modern speech patterns contain many negative invocations of energy. Most of the patterns are of self-hate, negative personal imaging and cursing of the self, the family, and the environment. "I hate that" and "d-mn it" are two classic examples. Without realizing it, the person who uses these two phrases sends hateful curses to people and things they might actually like and need in good working order.

The word "d-mn" has power and a definite meaning. We suggest that you revise your speech habits if you have been using this word. What a ridiculous mistake it is to say, "Well, I'll be d_mned."

An interesting example of secondary language and the reality of de-evolving humanity is the way some young people say that something is "bad" when they mean they like it. This is a prime example of complete distortion of language. If something pleases a person, it is certainly not "bad." Use of language such as this proves that the thought processes of the person speaking are seriously distorted.

We must realize that our thought/language circuit is somewhat of a closed loop. We program our unconscious minds with our speech patterns, and our speech patterns are controlled by the programs being run by our unconscious minds. We can, however, control our programming by being careful about how we use speech, and by being careful about what kind of subliminal messages we allow ourselves to be subjected to. We know that the subconscious is programmed by speech and thought patterns. This is why we use mantras and invocations or listen to audio hypnosis and subliminal tapes. We all have faith that repeating or listening to certain phrases has the power to affect our reality, if not our minds. What many people do not take into account, however, is that the music we listen to casually every day may have a powerful effect on our reality.

Perhaps we should start paying more attention to the programs the media attempts to put in our ears. Have you noticed that the lyrics of many rock and pop songs by popular artists contain powerful negative speech programs that are usually repeated over and over again? One example is the title of a hit song by a music superstar, "I'm Bad, I'm Bad." In fact, the words "I'm bad" are all there is to this song. The same words are repeated over and over to peppy, upbeat music. Another example is the pop, heavy-metal classic heard for the past several years on hard-rock stations titled, **"I Hate Myself for Loving You."** This song is a particularly good example of the mental poison being injected into America's ears. It is a deadly mantra which is combined with a hypnotic beat and repeated many, many times. No wonder so many people are messed up. They are being jammed with negative thought programs.

Lest you get the impression that this type of mental poisoning happens only in mainstream rock or heavy metal music, let us take note of a 1991, middle-of-the-road, soft-pop rock vocal hit, **"When Something is Wrong with My Baby, Something is Wrong with Me."** This rather questionable mantra is beautifully sung in a manner that totally disguises lyrics that are as questionable as those of the "bad" punk or heavy metal bands. Is this some kind of joke?

Do you allow subliminal messages to affect the way you look at life?

We must learn to use sound to both heal and activate the Earth.* When groups of people get together and chant or sing in a harmonious manner, they are sending balancing, harmonious energy into the energy grid of the planet. This type of work is always more powerful when done at power spots. In light of this, it is interesting to note that many, if not all, of the cathedrals in Europe are located on power spots. To activate the ascension program, we must come together in ceremony and send harmonious sound energy into the planetary grid.

The Earth produces low-frequency electromagnetic waves that occur just below the level of human perception (below 15 cycles per second). These low-frequency waves form a grid of *standing waves* on the Earth's surface. Due to the laws of harmonics, we know that the sound energy produced by chanting at power spots sends energy directly into the planetary grid. (E. J. Gurdjieff spoke of this in metaphysical terms many years ago.)

Simply chanting "OM" is very powerful and healing. OM means Love. Love is harmony. The Egyptian form of OM is AUM. If you have never chanted these sounds, I suggest you do so for at least ten minutes. You will then begin to understand what the yogis are talking about.

* *The Keys of Enoch* advises us to chant "Kodoish, Kodoish, Kodoish, Adonai 'Tsebayoth" (Holy, Holy, Holy, Lord God of Hosts) because this mantra is said to interconnect and create resonance among all levels of creation.

Sound is one of the most powerful transformational tools available to us. I have been experimenting with using sound in my ceremonies and meditations for several years, and I have found that simply intoning the vowel sounds or singing various words and phrases produces an effect on the body/mind that is quite noticeable, even to people who have little experience in working with energy.

As an example of the transformational power of sound as a tool of spiritual growth, I can look back on my own spiritual evolution and see that when I began experimenting with the "OM," I suddenly found that I could easily achieve an elevated state of consciousness that rapidly led me to greater spiritual insights and attunement to the Universal Life-Force Energies.

It is ironic that many Americans are not comfortable with singing, chanting, or toning (at least in public), as singing is certainly one of the most natural and healing things that we can do. Society's temporary loss of its singing abilities is apparently due to the fact that we have become dependent on recorded music to provide us with the much-needed spiritual food we refer to as music. And as we have become increasingly dependent on recorded music, we have allowed our natural desires and abilities to sing to fall into a high state of disuse.

This is most unfortunate, as these external sources of music do not provide for our much-needed internal experience of creating harmonious sound vibrations within our bodies. To make matters worse, we also find ourselves bombarded with music that is often far more agitating to our inner being than it is healing.

When considering the prospect of regaining our ability to heal ourselves with sound, we should remember that our ancestors, up to the most recent days, were very comfortable with singing. In fact, in "the old days" nearly everyone sang. Song was a part of everyone's life; even the most un-evolved peasants on the land had song as a part of everyday life.

One of the greatest gifts of organized religion has been its function of bringing communities together to create the harmonious vibrations of sacred song. And while many people have broken away from the Church for good reasons, the Earth suffers from the resulting lack of harmonizing sound vibrations that the congregations of old used to send to her regularly.

Let us remember that many, if not all, of the cathedrals, churches, and chapels in Europe were founded on power spots that were identified either by the priests or their predecessors, the pagan geomancers. Therefore, we can see how the harmonious sounds created in these areas were carried directly into the planetary grid. It is also interesting to note that Gothic cathedrals are built in the shape of a cross (which corresponds to the human form) and that the choir section corresponds to the throat chakra, which in the plan of these Cathedrals is just below the ten-sided "head" of the cross.

To regain the use of our natural ability to affect our environment with the use of sound, we must first remember that it is natural for humans to sing and chant, and that the main reason that many people do not do so on a regular basis is because we have allowed recorded music to take the place of our natural desire to produce and experience music. We can, however, regain control of our throat chakras (and have fun doing so) by practicing making sounds that are known to have power. The most basic of these sounds are the vowels, A,E,I,O,U (and the derivatives Ah and Eh). After you have become comfortable with using your voice you may well find that you will no longer be shy about using your voice in public.

INTONING VOWEL SOUNDS

In a place where you feel comfortable (safe), practice making each of the vowel sounds. When intoning each vowel, take a deep breath and hold the sound as long as is comfortable. Do one vowel at a time, repeating it over and over. As you do this take note of how you feel before and after intoning each vowel.

Also take note of how changing the shape of the lips a little, or using different positions of the tongue changes the sound of the vowel. Notice that the correct formation of each vowel is dependent on certain parameters of lip and tongue positioning: if you go beyond a certain limit you change into another vowel sound. You will find that "I," "A" and "AH" have very similar mouthings and that you must be focused on what you are actually intending to intone or you may find yourself making a different sound. (Professional singers practice this, and you may notice that some singers appear to be exaggerating their mouthings when in fact they are simply practicing their art.)

When experimenting with the vowel sounds be aware of the fact that you are engaging in an ancient and profound transformational technique: you are chanting. All of the sacred chants (mantras) that I am aware of rely heavily on the vowel sounds because, with the exception of the consonants H, L, M, N, R, and S these are the only sounds that can be sustained. As a result of this you will find that many mantric sounds rely on a combination of vowels with these consonants. It is interesting to note that by doing nothing more than intoning the vowels we can move quite a bit of energy through our bodies. This means that it is not necessary to recite phrases in Hebrew, Sanskrit or Native American that we do not understand.

Our verbal language is composed of a variety of sounds that correspond to letters. Our letters/sounds are understood to be of two varieties: vowels and consonants. Vowels are sounds that are produced by holding the tongue in a position that touches neither the top or bottom of the mouth. Consonants are distinguished by the fact that when pronouncing a consonant, the tongue will touch either the top or bottom of the mouth. This can be easily understood by speaking the vowel sounds A,E,I,O,U and noting the position of the tongue, and then by speaking any of the consonants.

THE ABILITY OF THE VOWELS TO ACTIVATE THE CHAKRAS

While it is commonly believed that the various vowel sounds activate the chakras, there is a great deal of debate as to which vowels activate which chakras, so I am including several diagrams showing some of the more commonly used systems. One of the problems I have with some of the modern systems is that some of them are in complete disagreement with the ancient teachings I am familiar with, such as the Tibetan system given in Lama Anagarika Govinda's *Foundations of Tibetan Mysticism*. What this means is that while the chakras themselves apparently have a distinct vibrational sound and seed syllable, as detailed in the Tibetan system, the sounds of the individual vowels can be applied to the chakras in different ways, and each system will produce a different result. It is important to note that the way individuals respond to the vowel sounds may have to do with either genetic inheritance, belief system, or soul origin.

One notable disagreement between the old and new systems is the sound associated with the heart chakra. In the Tibetan and east Indian systems, the seed syllable for the heart is "Hum" (or "Hu" for Eckankar). Modern systems, however, tend to place the "U" sounds in the lower chakras, assigning the sound "Ah" to the heart.

MORE NOTES ON THE POWER OF VOWEL SOUNDS

While I cannot claim to be a linguist of great or extensive knowledge, my research into this subject indicates that in the root languages which are the predecessors of English, such as Hebrew and Sanskrit, the vowels are singled out as having a vibrational power that contains important keys to accessing powerful universal energies. It is interesting to note that in the Hebrew language the vowels are not written, instead they are intimated by dots over the letters that compose the various words. I have been told that one of the original reasons for this is that the vowels are believed to have magical powers, and that it was thought to be improper to commit them to writing.

This lack of vowels in the construction of the written word makes Hebrew a particularly difficult language to learn, as one has to have a good working knowledge of the words themselves in order to know how to pronounce what is written, or to write what is to be pronounced. As for why we might be interested in using Hebrew or Sanskrit, rather than English, is that both of these languages have a profound connection to the formative energies of the universe itself.

These languages are "languages of Light" that are based on perfect waveforms of energy. Some very interesting discoveries have been made in relation to this, particularly the discovery that Golden Mean spirals expanded into three dimensions and viewed from 22 different angles, cast shadows that form the letters of the Hebrew alphabet. (My last book, *The Sedona UFO Connection*, had illustrations of this, but a dispute has arisen over the "ownership" of this research, so I will not be using these illustrations in this book. They were intriguing....) (See Key 215:63)

For more information about the Hebrew language as perfect waveforms of energy send a self-addressed stamped envelope to the Meru Foundation at P.O. Box 1738, San Anselmo, CA 94960, ask about the Geometric Metaphors of Life video.

Five Systems for Working With Vowel Sounds and the Chakras

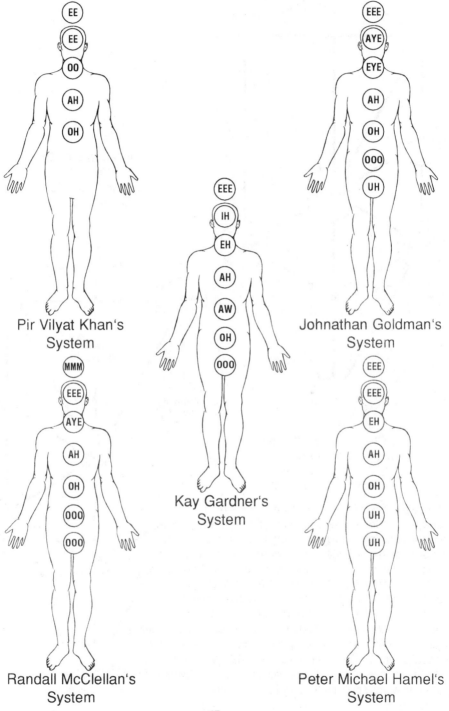

Pir Vilyat Khan's
System

Kay Gardner's
System

Johnathan Goldman's
System

Randall McClellan's
System

Peter Michael Hamel's
System

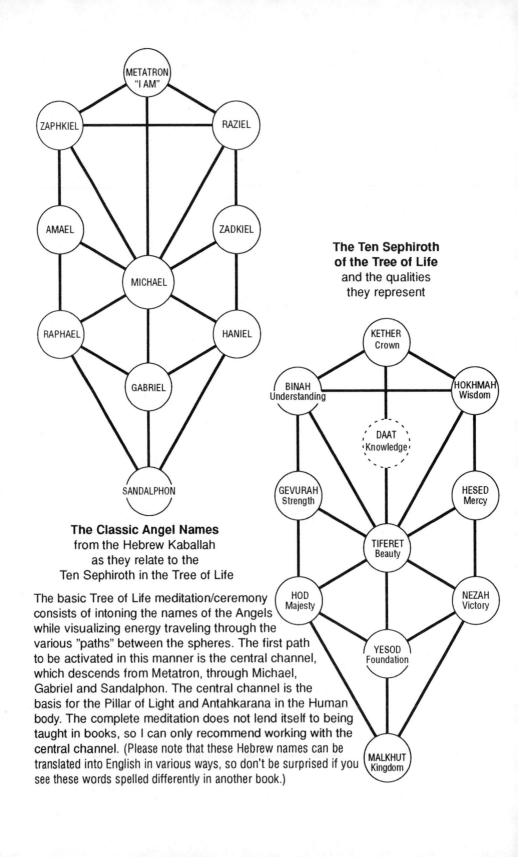

METATRON
"I AM"

ZAPHKIEL

RAZIEL

AMAEL

ZADKIEL

MICHAEL

RAPHAEL

HANIEL

GABRIEL

SANDALPHON

The Classic Angel Names
from the Hebrew Kaballah
as they relate to the
Ten Sephiroth in the Tree of Life

**The Ten Sephiroth
of the Tree of Life**
and the qualities
they represent

KETHER
Crown

BINAH
Understanding

HOKHMAH
Wisdom

DAAT
Knowledge

GEVURAH
Strength

HESED
Mercy

TIFERET
Beauty

HOD
Majesty

NEZAH
Victory

YESOD
Foundation

MALKHUT
Kingdom

The basic Tree of Life meditation/ceremony consists of intoning the names of the Angels while visualizing energy traveling through the various "paths" between the spheres. The first path to be activated in this manner is the central channel, which descends from Metatron, through Michael, Gabriel and Sandalphon. The central channel is the basis for the Pillar of Light and Antahkarana in the Human body. The complete meditation does not lend itself to being taught in books, so I can only recommend working with the central channel. (Please note that these Hebrew names can be translated into English in various ways, so don't be surprised if you see these words spelled differently in another book.)

In the western school of mysticism, the Hebrew language is used extensively because it is believed that Hebrew has a direct energetic/vibrational connection to the Universal Mind. What many students find, however, is that while Hebrew probably does have all the powers it is said to have, obtaining the proper pronunciations – hence the proper energy/vibrations is difficult unless one has a teacher who can work with them on a one-to-one basis.

In relation to this it is important to note that Dr. Hurtak, author of *The Keys of Enoch*, has developed pronunciations of certain Hebrew phrases that are sometimes quite different from those used by most people who speak the language. The difference is that Dr. Hurtak claims that the Master Enoch has instructed him in the original and proper pronunciations of these phrases, and that Hebrew as it is currently spoken has changed somewhat since the ancient days when the Master Enoch walked the Earth.

This can lead to quite a bit of confusion as one moves between circles of students, and one may find that Jewish people may be amazed, bewildered, amused, or angered by the way some of us use their language. One of the important distinctions between traditional Hebrew and Dr. Hurtak's pronunciations that are worthy of noting are that the Enoch-based pronunciation of the Hebrew letter Y is "Yud" in Hebrew and "Yod" in Enoch-based Hebrew. And, as far as I know, orthodox Jews do not usually say Yahweh, or YHWH, and it is considered most improper to do so. As far as I know, most traditional Jewish people refer to God as Elohim, Elohim-Adonai, or God.

As for the pronunciation of the word *Adonai*, this is another area where Dr. Hurtak's Enoch-based pronunciation differs from the mainstream. Using an English pronunciation for this spelling gives us a nice sounding word that comes off of the tongue easily. In the original Hebrew pronunciation, however, this is not the way it is said. Instead, all the vowels are accented, Ah-do-no-ee. As for the pronunciation of the sacred mantra *Kodoish, Kodoish, Kodoish, Adonai 'Tsebayoth*, the more commonly accepted pronunciation is **Kodosh, Kodosh, Kodosh, Ah-do-no-ee, Sabayot.**

In closing this part of the discussion I will simply state that for many people it might be somewhat counterproductive to attempt to learn Hebrew words without verbal instruction, so I suggest that we stick with sounds and phrases that we can all learn easily, such as the vowels and certain "seed syllables" from Sanskrit that are based on the vowels Om, Hum, Ah, Ram, etc. It is also interesting to note that shamanic traditions around the world, including those of the Native Americans, rely heavily on the vowel sounds for their chants.

ANGEL NAMES AND ALOHA

Many people do not realize it, but the names we commonly use for the Archangels: Michael, Gabriel, Uriel, and Raphael are actually mispronunciations of the original Hebrew names! People who study the Tree of Life teachings of the Kabbalah (spell that one any way you like) are convinced that those who are uninitiated into the Hebrew language cannot properly invoke the Angels because they do not know how to properly vibrate their names. While I am not totally convinced that this is an absolute fact, I do feel that it is helpful to attempt to use the proper pronunciations. Once again, however, we find that without direct oral instruction it is difficult to impart this knowledge. Nonetheless, let's give it a try:

Michael	Meek-I-a-el
Gabriel	Gah-vre-el
Uriel	Oo-ree-el (oo as in moon)
Raphael	Rah-fi-el (i as in I)

Key 217:83 of The Keys of Enoch refers to these four entities as the "the collective Pillar of Light." It is highly desirable to intone these names during the Merkaba/Medicine Wheel ceremonies. This is basically the same thing that pagans and Native Americans do when they "call in the directions" or "call in the Grandfathers."

William Grey, one of the most noted Kabbalists of modern times, assigns the following qualities to the vowel sounds:

A	-	Earth	-	North
E	-	Air	-	East
I	-	Fire	-	South
O	-	Water	-	West
U	-	Ether		

ALOHA

One of my favorite words of power is "aloha," which I am told means love in Hawaiian. It is my belief that this word one of the most powerful words we can use to call in Angelic helpers and invoke the power of Universal Love. One of my favorite practices is to invoke the Pillar of Light and then chant aloha. I frequently use this technique when I work with groups. When I chant aloha, I find that my energies become balanced and I become more open to Universal Life-Force Energies.

In the language the Master Christ spoke, Aramaic, one of the names of God used by the Master was Allaha, a phrase with an almost identical vibrational quality as aloha. In Aramaic, Allaha is also very similar in pronunciation to the singular form of Elohim, "Eloha" (Eh-low-ha). Elohim is considered by orthodox jews to be one of the names of God. Students of The Keys of Enoch and other New Age teachings feel that Elohim is not the name of the Absolute Source, that it is instead a name for very high entities that create the worlds of manifestation, in harmony with the Will of the Supreme Creator.

I refer those who are interested in learning more about sound to *The Cosmic Octave* by Hans Cousto, which can be ordered through any metaphysical bookstore. Mr. Cousto obviously knows quite a bit about sound, and he has developed interesting formulas for calculating the resonant frequencies of our planet as well as other planets in our system.

On page 32 of his book he refers to natural electromagnetic frequencies (spherics) in our atmosphere that have a harmonic relation to musical sound and the octave, corresponding to the laws of musical proportion (see illustration). The frequency of our planet's rotation also plays a role in the production of the spherics.

On page 37 of the same book we find that the well-known genetic researcher Fritz Popp of the Kaiserslautern University in West Germany has determined that DNA has a resonant frequency that has a direct relation to the *66th* harmonic of the frequency of the Earth's rotation! This high frequency has to do with the scientifically recognized ability of DNA to communicate on the molecular level with light. In other words, when strands of DNA break apart during replication, they emit ultraviolet light, which encodes the DNA/RNA molecules in the nucleus.

Another naturally occurring frequency we should be aware of is the *Earth wave* or Schuman resonance, which occurs between 7-8 cycles per second. By dividing the speed of light of 186,282 mps by the Earth's average diameter of 24,880 statute miles, we arrive at a frequency of 7.49 cps, which is close to the average frequency of the Earth wave – 7.8 cps. (Variations in the atmosphere apparently slow the transmission of these waves, thus raising the frequency slightly.) This frequency is in the range of theta brainwaves, which are known to accompany exotic altered states of consciousness, such as out-of-body experiences. This means that when we resonate with the Earth we have the opportunity to transcend the limits of physical reality.

These natural electromagnetic waves in the atmosphere are the direct result of pulses of energy that are constantly being injected into the Earth's atmosphere by the average of 2,000 lightning strikes per minute that occur around the planet. The electrons that cause these lightning strikes come to this planet from the Sun, via the *solar wind*. They have been captured by the Earth's magnetic field, which, in turn, releases them into the ionosphere. Ultimately, these electrons make their way into the clouds, which discharge them into the Earth in the form of lightning. This phenomenon should be considered an important element in our understanding of our planet's energy grid.

You can see an illustration of the Earth's electromagnetic field and the solar wind in the section of this book on the planetary grid.

Modern science has discovered that the harmonic relationships of music, as defined by Pythagoras, can be seen in the formation of physical matter. Taking this concept a step further, Drunvalo Melchizedek claims that the dimensions (the third, fourth, fifth, etc.) are also arranged harmonically according to the principles discovered by Pythagoras. (Key 303:47 alludes to this.)

The question arises: What constitutes a dimension? According to the *Keys of Enoch*, each universe is a "complete electromagnetic spectrum." From this we can infer that each dimension is a vibrational node in the unified field. As Drunvalo Melchizedek points out in his Flower of Life workshop, science has determined that there is a background of microwave radiation found throughout deep space that has a wavelength of 7.23 centimeters. This is apparently the resonant frequency of what we refer to as the third dimension.

One of the easiest ways to conceptualize the vibrational relationship between the dimensions is to study the keyboard of a piano. An octave on the keyboard consists of 13 keys – eight white and five black. The notes of the keys are proportioned harmonically, using a mathematic formula that is attributed to Pythagoras. Each of the vibrational nodes of the octave, or "notes" can be seen as representing a dimension. (See illustration page 72.)

Each dimension is a vibrational node in the unified field. What we can infer from this is that the higher dimensions exist in an energy state that has a higher frequency than our own dimension. This tells us that travel between dimensions is a process of raising or lowering frequency (vibration).

As we gain energy through the practice of the Merkaba meditation we will gain the ability to spiral our Merkaba fields at velocities that approach the speed of light. As this happens, the matter that forms our physical bodies will increase in frequency and pass through the energy threshold that separates our dimension from the higher vibrational realms.

The concept of thresholds separating the dimensions is an important aspect of interdimensional travel that should be understood by anyone attempting this variety of exploration. I refer to these thresholds as "membranes." I got this term from the *Keys of Enoch*, and while I am not certain that Dr. Hurtak would agree with my definition, my experiences in interdimensional travel have shown me that there is a phenomenon that could aptly be described as a membrane that separates interdimensional energy states.

As humans moves between dimensions or energy states, they have to pass through the membranes that separate these energy states. Because of this the passage through a membrane can be compared to a quantum jump: a specific amount of energy/vibration must be acquired in order to make this passage, and when it is made the transition is quite clearly experienced and noted.

The first membrane that every human encounters is their own body. The body is the membrane that separates the individual human from the rest of the universe. The body is what defines a human in the third dimension. When a human dreams or has an out-of-body experience, they pass through the membrane of the physical body, carrying with them their mental body and perhaps aspects of their etheric body.

I have experienced these interdimensional membranes, and I consider this experience to be one of the most important events in my life, as I was able to witness how the pure energy/language of the Universal Creator passes through a membrane into this dimension to create what we call reality. This was quite a revelation, and I assure you that this primal God-force is language – the language of Light – I have seen it. This experience also helped illustrate how multiple dimensions occupy the same space.

The concept of multiple dimensions occupying the same space has been one of the things that has led many members of the scientific community to dismiss the notion of multiple dimensions. It defies logic to imagine that there could be multiple realities in the same space. Yet, while this seems impossible, I have had experiences that indicate this is a fact. The best explanation I have found for the maintenance of multiple dimensions is that there is a primal energy state in our universe that exists in a dimensional phase that is somehow parallel to all dimensions, and that this primal dimension of pure energy/language manifests multiple dimensions simultaneously in the same space. Each dimension can be compared to a musical note: a node in the unified field. A good analogy for this is Metatron's Cube – the central circle is able to be in direct contact with six other circles simultaneously. (Taking Metatron's Cube off two-dimensional paper and constructing it in three dimensions puts the central sphere in contact with 12 independent spheres.

(12+1= 13)

I have found that science has identified various phenomena that apparently reveal that there is a primal energy state in the universe that exists outside the threshold of physical manifestation. In regard to this I refer the reader to the April 1989 issue of *Scientific American*, page 56. I believe that the Aharonov-Bohm Effect described in this article is evidence of the primal dimension of pure energy that fuels all electromagnetic fields in our dimension, including the Kundalini and Pranic energy phases.

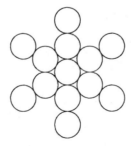

METATRON'S CUBE

Are the Dimensions Harmonically Arranged According to the Laws of Musical Proportion?

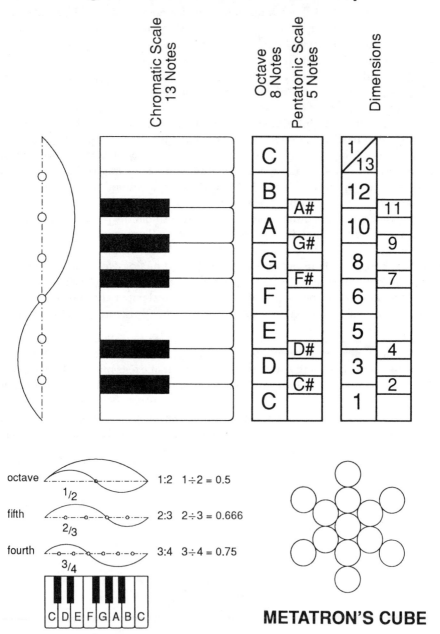

The 13th note is twice the frequency of the first note of the octave; it is also the first note of the next octave. Because of this, the 13th note occupies the interesting position of being in two octaves at once, and being both the first and final note of an octave. It is therefore, in a manner of speaking, the Alpha and Omega.

We send our prayers to the Most High Holy Spirit.

Oh Great Spirit, we ask to be shown how to access the sacred energies which you send us, and we ask that our prayers be heard.

We invoke the Holy Spirit. We ask that a pillar of this Infinite Light be placed over us.

We ask that the Divine Archangels of the Highest and Most Holy Spirit be here with us now.

We ask that the Master Jesus Christ be here with us now.

Guide us and protect us, great Masters.

We now cancel, nullify, and dissolve the evil which tries to enslave us and keep us in darkness.

We ask to be shown how to access the Light of Ascension.

We ask for the activation of the Light workers.

We ask for further activation of the planetary Light Body, and for the healing of the planet itself.

We ask for the return of the Christ.

We pray for peace on our planet.

May all be healed.

We send healing Christ energy to our fellow human beings and ask that every human heart be opened to the way of Love and Christ Consciousness.

In the name of the Most High we ask these things,

And may these things we have called for begin now.

We invoke the mighty I AM Presence.

We invoke the Divine Light and the Sacred Fire.

We are in alignment with the Divine Light and the Sacred Fire.

We ask that our bodies be transformed by the Divine Light and the Sacred Fire.

Purify, purify, purify.

We are Light, we are Light, we are Light.

We are Love, we are Love, we are Love.

We call for the transformation of this planet into a higher dimensional phase of total alignment with the Christ energies.

We call for the return of the Christ.

We ask that our space brothers and sisters make themselves known to us, and that they assist us in planetary transformation.

We send Light and Love to the entire planet.

And so it is

on all dimensions,

Universes within Universes,

worlds within worlds.

Our prayer is heard

And Spirit responds.

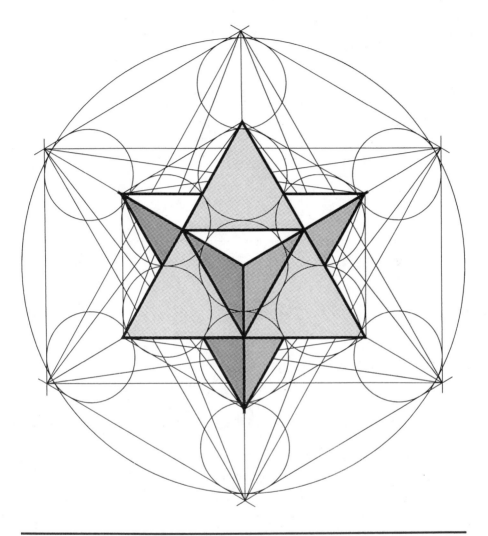

The Shaded Figure is the "Star Tetrahedron" of the Merkaba

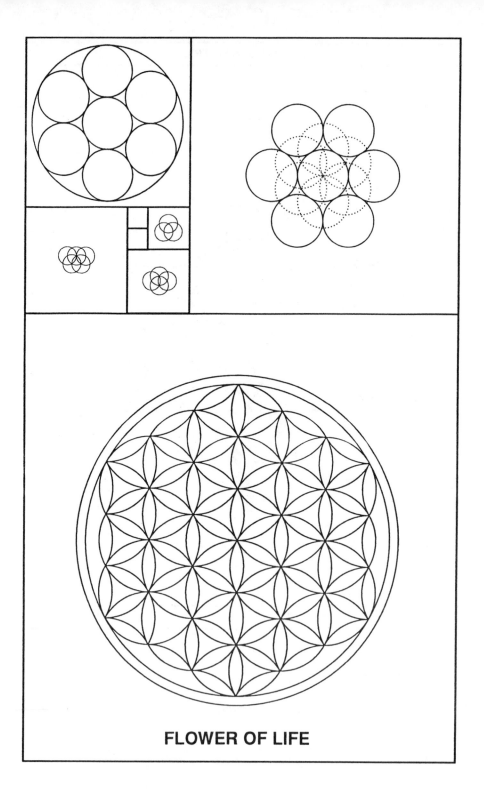

FLOWER OF LIFE

There is no limit as to what can be understood through the study of sacred geometry, as this science explores and explains the web of energy that creates and unifies all things. There is a limit, however, as to what can be said about sacred geometry in any one book, as the subject is vast beyond belief, containing countless levels and interconnections that could take lifetimes to explore. (We will therefore only review some of the basic concepts that relate to the process of ascension and the Vortex phenomenon.)

When we study sacred geometry we are allowed a glimpse of the inner workings of the Universal Mind of God. The originator of the term "philosopher," Pythagoras, believed the study of these geometrics and their related subjects to be of the highest importance, as these studies reveal the inner workings of the Universe itself. He believed that this study of God, as the universe, was essential to the education of the soul.

The word "sacred" has many meanings. Originally this word referred only to things that were absolute and permanent, because that which is absolute and permanent is of God. The energy patternings of sacred geometry are what *The Keys of Enoch* refer to as "Threshold Commands" (from the Throne of God). Threshold Commands control the entire spectrum of universal creation, from the superelectron to DNA.

Archaeological evidence proves that these concepts have been understood and revered by all wisdom-holders in Western culture from at least as far back in time as ancient Egypt. If the theory of reincarnation is correct, then many of us who are drawn to this form of philosophical research are in the process of remembering what we studied in previous lifetimes.

The basic mathematic principles of sacred geometry are not overly complex, and any high school graduate should have no problem understanding them. I suggest that you go over this material with a calculator, a pencil, and a piece of paper. Look the drawings over carefully and you will find intriguing correspondences between the various geometric, mathematic, and harmonic concepts.

Many people find these concepts fascinating and empowering, as they demonstrate that the Universe, our planet, and our bodies are not random events created out of nothingness, but rather an intelligent formation of energy patternings that appear to be evidence of a primal universal Intelligence that may be referred to as God.

According to Pythagoras the science of number was the basis for all things. Each of the numbers: 1,2,3,4,5,6,7,8,9, 10 are seen to be an essence and universal vibration unto themselves.

ARITHMETIC – Number in itself.

GEOMETRY – Number in space. Geometry originally meant "to measure the Earth."

MUSIC and HARMONICS – Number in time.

ASTRONOMY – Number in space and time.

Seed of life crop formation, taken in 1994 by Mellerstain Gordon, the Earl of Haddington, Great Britain

The Seed of Life is the core of **Metatron's Cube**, an object that is an essential element of universal geometrics, as it contains all energy patterns necessary for the production of the Platonic Solids. (See page 81.)

Metatron's Cube represents a primary grouping of 13 independent circles within the Flower of Life. (See Buckminster Fuller's *Synergetics II* for information about the formation of three-dimensional objects from 13 spheres.)

For more information on crop circles in the United States and overseas, send a self-addressed stamped envelope to:

CENTRE FOR CROP CIRCLE STUDIES
US NETWORK
P.O. BOX 900
TENINO, WA 98589

(360) 264-4544

ilyes@earthlink.net

GENESIS OF ALL FORM

1

2

3

4

5

6

7 SEED OF LIFE

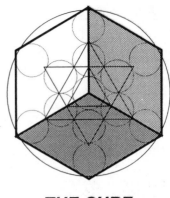

THE CUBE

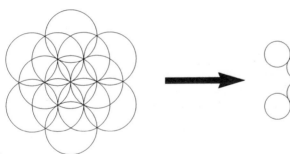

EGG OF LIFE

METATRON'S CUBE

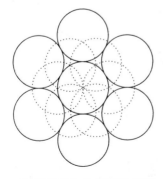

SEVEN CIRCLES

FLOWER OF LIFE

Platonic Solids

These primal 3-dimensional objects are completely symmetrical, each object is composed of 1 angle, identical faces, and equal side lengths.

	Edges	Faces	Vertices	Length
Tetrahedron - Fire				
	6	4	4	$\sqrt{2}$
Octahedron - Air				
	12	8	6	$\dfrac{1}{\sqrt{2}}$
Cube - Earth				
	12	6	8	1
Icosahedron - Water - Biological Life Force				
	30	20	12	Φ
Dodecahedron - Ether - Universal Life Force				
	30	12	20	$1/\Phi$

Generation of Platonic Solids From Seed of Life and Metatron's Cube

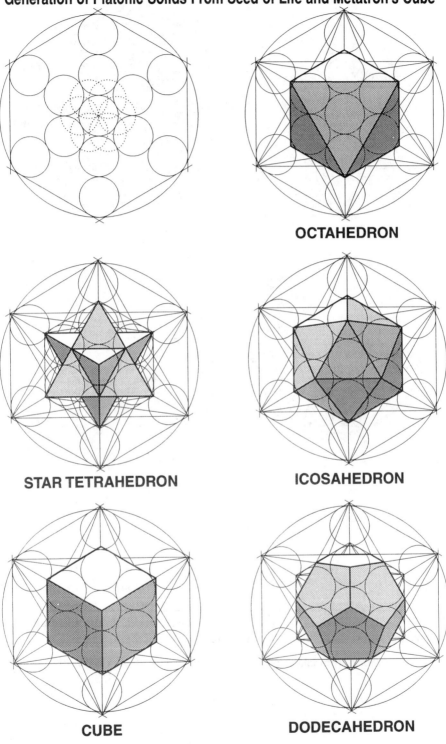

OCTAHEDRON

STAR TETRAHEDRON

ICOSAHEDRON

CUBE

DODECAHEDRON

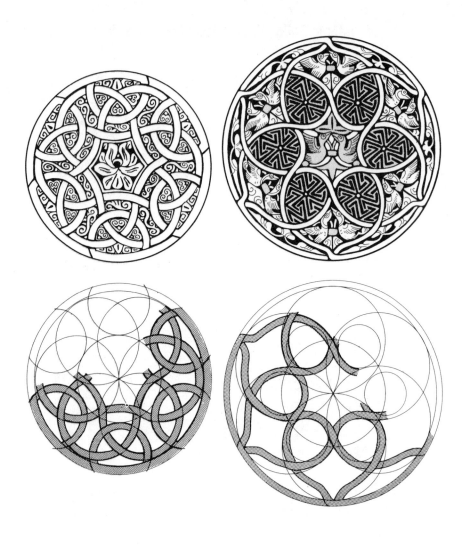

The seven-circle design is well know in the Muslim world. In this illustration we can see the seven-circles are the underlying structure of these designs.

Illustration from Islamic Designs, by Eve Wilson, Dover Publications

*A THREE-DIMENSIONAL
FLOWER OF LIFE IN THE
GRIP OF A STONE LION
OUTSIDE THE EMPEROR'S
PRIVATE RESIDENCE IN
THE FORBIDDEN CITY,
BEIJING, CHINA*

Those who are familiar with Chinese culture will recall the fact that stone lions similar to this one are found throughout China, and that the builders of various oriental temples often placed stone lions at the thresholds of sacred sites to be symbolic guardians of the mysteries of the "heavenly realms." Many students of esoteric thought consider these stone lions to be somewhat equivalent to the many Sphinx sculptures that are found in Egypt. It should be noted that the archetype of the lion is associated with the Sun and the mysteries of transformation into the Body of Light.

This photograph has found its way into the second edition of this book, courtesy of the photographer Ilizabeth Fortune. Ilizabeth has studied with Drunvalo Melchizedek since 1988. She is a popular teacher of the Flower of Life, and she also specializes in Dolphin Swims.

**Ilizabeth Fortune; (707) 485-1205 – Fax (707) 485-1408
1190 N. State St. #311 Ukiah, CA 95482**

You can see a close-up view of the spherical flower of life on page 121

The Father's Divine Eye is the pattern of creation behind the creation. (Key 316:5)

The "petals" of the Flower of Life form a symbol that is well known to most Christians: the vesica piscis, or "fish." This symbol has quite a bit of esoteric meaning and genuine power as part of the Threshold Commands that form our reality. The vesica piscis reveals the root of all Vortex phenomenon throughout the universe. By understanding these things the student will be brought to an understanding of the universal nature of the Vortex. (See illustration of vesica piscis.)

The common explanation for this symbol is that it is used to symbolize the power of manifestation that the Master Christ exhibited when he fed a large gathering of people by turning a few fish and loaves of bread into enough food to feed everyone present. Going a level deeper, we also see the fish that the Master produced as a sacrament, or divine food, was created by act of magic: complete control of physical reality. Therefore, the symbol of the fish also symbolizes the divine spiritual food and universal abundance the faithful are invited to partake of as we achieve Christ Consciousness.

Various writings and works of art produced by early Christians indicate that some of their sects associated the mysteries of the Master Christ with dolphins, not fish. Over the centuries, however, the correlation between the Master Christ and dolphins was slowly lost, and because of the numerous references to fish in the New Testament, the consciousness concept represented by the dolphin was ultimately replaced by the symbol of the fish.*

Another interpretation of the vesica piscis is that the two circles represent Heaven and Earth or spirit and matter, and that the area where they join is symbolic of the universal function of the Christ as mediator between these realms. It can therefore be said that the vesica piscis represents both duality and unity.

Perhaps most importantly, however, the petals of the Flower of Life are also associated with the symbol known as the "All-Seeing Eye of God." Students of *The Keys of Enoch* will no doubt find this concept particularly intriguing as the *Keys* are primarily concerned with Metatronic science, which has to do primarily with understanding the formation of the universe.

In Drunvalo Melchizedek's Flower of Life course he gives a very good explanation of how the structure of light waves and the human eye can be shown to have a direct relation to the geometries of the vesica piscis.

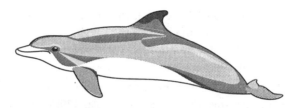

* In our current era we once again find the dolphin being used to symbolize consciousness expansion, harmony with the universe, and the process of ascension. (As well as extraterrestrial consciousness from the star Sirius – see Robert Temple's book *The Sirius Mystery*).

The Vesica Piscis, the "Eye of God"

And The Three "Sacred Roots" at the Eye of the Vortex

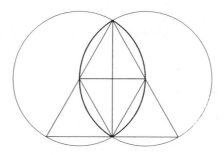

Pythagoras discovered that the square roots of the numbers 2, 3, 5 are fundamental properties that are present in the creation of all form.

These three square roots are found in the Vesica Piscis.

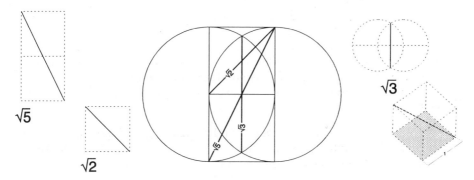

This illustration shows the relation of the three "sacred roots."

The square root of 2 defines the diagonal of the square. Its quality is generation. $\sqrt{2}$ = 1.4142135...

The square root of 3 defines both the diagonal of a cube and the long diagonal of the Vesica Piscis. Its quality is formation of three dimensional space. $\sqrt{3}$ = 1.7320508...

The square root 5 defines the Golden Rectangle and the Golden Mean proportion or Φ. Its quality is regeneration, or growth. It is seen to represent the life-giving qualities of the Christ. $\sqrt{5}$ = 2.2360679...

THE FIBONACCI AND GOLDEN MEAN SPIRALS AS THE
PRIMARY ENERGY PATTERNS FOR ALL VORTEX FORMATION

The Fibonacci and Golden Mean spirals are almost identical to one another. The difference being that Golden Mean rectangles are in an exact 1:618 ratio (having a diagonal of the square root of 5), whereas Fibonacci rectangles are produced by simple multiplication beginning with a single base square. The Fibonacci set is nature's way of creating the Golden Mean using whole numbers.

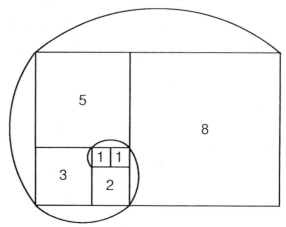

Leonardo Fibonacci was a thirteenth-century mathematician. The Fibonacci set describes, in whole numbers, the Golden Mean ratio, which is 1:618.... This numerical sequence is one of the most important concepts in sacred geometry and conventional physics..

This sequence of numbers is commonly found in organic growth patterns. Because of this we can see another direct relation between the pentagram and life: all the line segments of the pentagram are in exact Golden Mean ratios.

This sequence consists of simple addition, beginning with 1+1.
1+1=2; 1+2=3; 2+3=5; 3+5=8; 5+8=13; 8+13=21; 13+21=34; 21+34=55; 34+55=89; 55+89=144, etc. to infinity. (144 is the *12th* number in the sequence.)

The Fibonacci sequence's relation to the Golden Mean can be demonstrated through the use of division. Please note that the results get closer to 1.618 as the numbers get higher.
1/1=1; 2/1=2; 3/2=1.5; 5/3=1.666; 8/5=1.6; 13/8=1.625; 21/13=1.615

It is easy to read a great deal of symbolism into the geometrical form generated by the Fibonacci set, particularly the first three functions:
1= Unity, 2= Duality, 3= Trinity

To this we could add that the vesica piscis can fit over these squares perfectly, thus showing that the three "sacred roots" are present in this form from the beginning. Pythagoras referred to the square as "the key of nature." This is the basis for Universal Vortex formation.

The Ratios of Musical Proportion

"The Fifth"

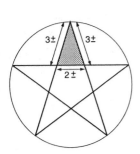

2:3 - corresponds to
the sides of the
pentagram's triangle,
which approximates
the ratio 2:3.
2 ÷ 3 = 0.666

"The Fourth"

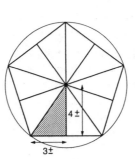

3:4 - corresponds to
the sides of the
pentagon's triangle.
3 ÷ 4 = 0.75

"The Octave"

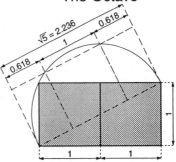

1:2 - corresponds to a
rectangle composed of two
squares with a diagonal of
2.236, which is √5.

octave 1:2 1÷2 = 0.5

The fifth closest approximates
the perfect golden mean ratio
or Φ phi which is 1.618....

fifth 2:3 2÷3 = 0.666

fourth 3:4 3÷4 = 0.75

The black & white keys represent the
ratios of musical proportion.

There are 8 white and 5 black keys.
     8 : 5 = 1.6 — 5 : 8 = 0.625

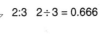

C D E F G A B C

The black keys are in groups of 2
and 3. The series 2 : 3 : 5 : 8 is part
of the Fibonacci series. All these
ratios come close to Φ, which is 1.618.

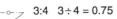

5   8:5   8÷5 = 1.6

8

Just as some of these dimensions and proportions are approximate (+ or -)
values, it should be remembered that there is no "perfect" tuning for the piano.
Variance is part of nature. If everything were numerically and geometrically
exact, reality would be crystalized in time.

The Pentagram

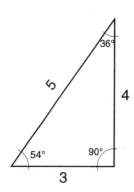

The 3 - 4 - 5 triangle is a natural component of the pentagram.

This traingle is used as a basic design unit for megalithic sites around the world, including Stonehenge.

The triangles of the UVG planetary grid are in almost identical in proportion to the classic 3 - 4 - 5 triangle you see illustrated here.

Eight UVG triangles can be combined to create a scale replica that will duplicate the exact angles of the Great Pyramid.

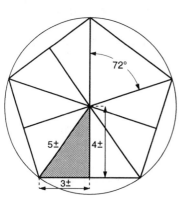

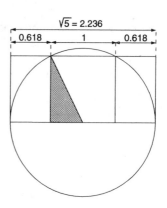

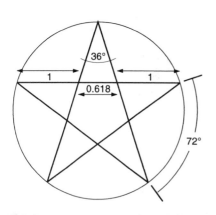

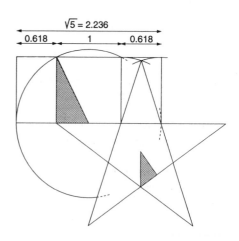

Each line segment of the five pointed star is in perfect Golden Mean proportion, in relation to the other lines.

The pentagram was adopted by the ancient philosophers as the symbol of knowledge of the mysteries of creation. They also associated the pentagram with light. All line segments in the pentagram are in perfect Golden Mean proportion. This is one of the primary reasons the ancients adopted this symbol to represent the mysteries they studied.

Pentagonal geometries manifest naturally only in biological systems. The geometries of the pentagon act as a waveguide or antenna for the specific varieties of life-force energy that create biological life. Non-organic materials, such as crystals and rocks, never exhibit natural crystallization patterns that are based on pentagonal geometrics.

The primary angle of the pentagram is 72 degrees (360 divided by 5 equals 72). This is half of 144, which is a fractal of the light harmonic. The pentagram's geometries act as a waveguide/antenna for the Universal Life-Force Energies that create biological life. The outer angles of the pentagon in the core of the pentagram are 144 degrees.

The pentagram is one of the basic components of the icosahedron, which is one of the basic components of the UVG grid.

DNA – Genetic material is composed of a lattice of interlocking pentagrams that create a geometrical form known as a *ratcheted dodecahedron*. The dodecahedron is formed by 12 pentagrams. Various well-known channels have stated that as we "activate our light codes" our DNA will develop 12 strands.

According to Lawrence Blair, in his book, *Rhythms of Vision*, the ratcheting dodecahedron of DNA "ratchets" 10 times to make a complete turn. Each segment of the turn will therefore be separated by 36 degrees, which is also harmonically related to 144,000. Thirty six reduces to 9. All angles in the pentagram also reduce to 9.

The military headquarters of the United States is a pentagon that is aligned with the North Star, **and** very closely aligned, on the north-south axis to the planetary grid node in the Bermuda triangle (point 18). This north-south grid line also goes through Southeast Asia (Vietnam, Laos, Cambodia, and Thailand).

Tree of Life and Flower of Life
as they relate to the Human figure

FROM CHAOS CONSCIOUSNESS TO CHRIST CONSCIOUSNESS: THE MERKABA, VORTEX TECHNOLOGY, AND THE MEDICINE WHEEL

I have taken a great deal of inspiration for this book from the work of Drunvalo Melchizedek and his Flower of Life workshop. Like many other people, I originally came to know Drunvalo and the Flower of Life teachings through a set of bootleg video tapes that were released through one of his students. These amazing video tapes, though poor in visual quality, contain such profound information about ascension that by the power of their own essence they were copied and circulated throughout the country.

These tapes represent one of the most interesting phenomena that have occurred to date in the New Age consciousness movement, as they explain in detail the mechanics of ascension and how each individual human can access Christ Consciousness energies through the practice of the Merkaba meditation. As a demonstration of the profound power of the Flower of Life material, hundreds of people who saw the bootleg tapes for free in their homes later signed up to take the Flower of Life training for the full price of $444. At this point, in the spring of 1995, interest in Drunvalo's work continues to increase, and Drunvalo has become so busy that he has not been able to fulfill the demand for a book on the Flower of Life.

Most of what Drunvalo teaches is ancient knowledge that cannot be said to be the property of any individual on this planet, so there is no reason why anyone called to teach these techniques cannot do so, providing, of course, that they can handle the shamanic realities that come with being a teacher of such powerful techniques. Therefore, I want to make it clear that I am not ripping off Drunvalo's material, and that I am in fact writing about the Flower of Life with Drunvalo's blessing. The Flower of Life material in this book is distilled through my own consciousness and is an extension of the work I have been engaged in for some time. Students of Drunvalo's work will be able to see that this book represents a teaching that stands on its own, which is in harmony with what Drunvalo presents.

The goal of the Flower of Life workshop is to learn how to achieve Christ Consciousness through the study of sacred geometry and the practice of the Merkaba meditation. This meditation is a visualization and breath technique that activates the interlocking light cones (tetrahedrons) of the human Light Body. In the advanced stages of this meditation the student is taught how to gain control of these light cones, and make them rotate, thus creating an individual Merkaba/Vortex, that, when fully functional will automatically take the student into the Christ Consciousness dimension.

Christ Consciousness is a state of existence that represents complete harmony with the universe. As the Light Body is activated and energized with the breath techniques taught in the Flower of Life workshop, students develop the ability to make their Light Body rotate at high speed. This takes the student beyond the random chaos consciousness of our current level of existence, and into a state of existence of full resonance with the basic energy patterns of the universe. The universal energy of Love is a key element in this practice.

The Merkaba is an advanced technique that does not lend itself well to being taught through a book. Therefore, only the basic principles will be given here. The breath and visualization techniques are moderately complex, and I think that it would be counterproductive for most students to attempt to go directly into these techniques without having first spent some time working on the basic techniques of using the Pillar of Light and the Antahkarana to draw the Holy Spirit (Universal Life-Force Energy) into the body and allowing it to expand in the heart. (When you are ready for the more advanced techniques, I suggest that you take the Flower of Life workshop or attend one of my own classes.)

One of the most inspiring aspects of the Flower of Life workshop is the information Drunvalo shares about his contact with Angels and the Ascended Master Thoth. It is from these entities that Drunvalo learned that each human has a precise, etheric Light grid that manifests around the body as a star tetrahedron. (This form can be described as a three-dimensional Star of David.) Interdimensional travel and focus in the various dimensions (or "assemblage" – see Carlos Castaneda's work) is controlled by the frequency of the rotation of the star tetrahedron.

The star tetrahedron light grid of the Merkaba has three aspects. Two of these aspects rotate in opposite directions while the third holds the focus by remaining stationary. Originally, when I first saw the bootleg tapes, I did not understand how this worked. I thought that the star tetrahedron only had one aspect and that its top and bottom tetrahedrons rotated independently of one another in opposite directions. This, however, is not correct.

The Merkaba, as explained by Drunvalo Melchizedek under the guidance of the Ascended Master Thoth, is composed of a star tetrahedron that has three aspects. The primary aspect always remains stationary, as the reference for its other two aspects that rotate in opposite directions.

In the Merkaba meditation, the two aspects of the star tetrahedron that rotate are separated through an act of *Will* and made to rotate in opposite directions. The key to gaining control of these star tetrahedrons is to develop personal power through the use of the Pillar of Light and the Antahkarana.

The various spiritual exercises given in this book will assist you in preparing for the Merkaba meditation. As you work with the Pillar of Light and the Antahkarana, it is helpful to visualize the light grid of the star tetrahedron that surrounds the body. For men, one of the ridges of the upward-pointing tetrahedron runs along the front of the body, for women, this ridge will go up the back. As long as these two "Light cones" remain stationary, the physical body consciousness remains focused in the third dimension. When students learn the Merkaba meditation they gain the ability to separate their star tetrahedrons into two identical and independent units that rotate in opposite directions. (See illustrations.)

In the study of sacred geometry the star tetrahedron stands out as a unique object that naturally nests inside the cube, the icosahedron, and the dodecahedron. Because of this the star tetrahedron is seen as a quality that *generates* these primal forms. (See illustration of Platonic Solids in Metatron's Cube.)

One of the things that is so interesting about Drunvalo Melchizedek's Flower of Life workshop is the high level of resonance most of the participants have with the information he presents. It is, as he tells his students at the beginning of the class, if I may take the liberty of paraphrasing him, "I am not teaching you anything you do not already know; I am only helping you remember. The concepts contained within the Flower of Life are within you already".

The interlocking circle design of the Flower of Life has the ability to unlock memories that are deep within our being because it is a primary energy/language pattern that has a resonance with all things within us and around us. The Flower of Life should be considered to be a power symbol, which, when studied activates energy codings in the mind that help the student access their Light Body/Merkaba. I suggest that you spend some time looking at the illustration which shows how the Flower of Life relates to both the human figure and the Kabbalistic/Egyptian teaching of the Tree of Life. (The Tree of Life is one of the most ancient and profound teachings of the awareness of Universal Life-Force Energies and the Light Body.)

In the Flower of Life workshop Drunvalo shows photographs he has gathered from around the world that indicate that the Flower of Life was known and revered by many ancient mystic sects. It is quite interesting to see that the ancient Egyptians painted the Flower of Life onto the columns of the temple of Osiris in Abydos, Egypt, and that a temple at Masada, Israel, has a mosaic of the Flower of Life in the middle of the floor in the main room. But undoubtedly the most amazing photograph that Drunvalo has of the Flower of Life is the three-dimensional sculpture of it clutched in the paws of one of the stone lions that guard the Emperor's residence inside the Forbidden Palace in Beijing, China!

In the summer of 1995, the seven-circle design, which is the basis for the Flower of Life, *appeared as a crop circle* in the fields of northern England. (See photo.) In sacred geometry, this pattern of seven interlocking circles is known as the **Seed of Life**. It is considered to be the basic unit of information necessary for the formation of all material substance. According to Drunvalo's research this figure also has a direct relation to the formation of light waves.

FLOWER OF LIFE CLASSES

FLOWER OF LIFE RESEARCH, INC.
1618 E. BELL RD. #106 • PHOENIX, AZ 85022
(602) 996-0900 • http://www.FlowerofLife.org

Our galaxy, the stars, our solar system, our planet, the Vortices of planet Earth and the human body are all aspects of the spiraling energies of the universal Merkaba.

When I wrote my first book, *Sedona Power Spot, Vortex and Medicine Wheel Guide,* I spent many hours musing over the concept of spiraling energy. At that point I was still fairly new to this field and I did not have as much information as I do today. I had been told that it was safe to work only with spiraling energy that moved in a clockwise direction, and that counterclockwise energy fields were "negative," "dangerous," and "used by black magicians." Since that time, and with the help of various teachers, including Drunvalo Melchizedek, I have come to the realization that what I had been taught about the "dangers" of counterclockwise energy fields and the superiority of clockwise energy fields was for the most part superstitious rubbish that has no basis in metaphysical truth.

The universe is in balance. The study of Universal Merkaba/Vortex phenomenon shows us that the mirror-twin energy fields sustain one another. Neither the right nor the left are "good" or "evil," as these concepts are entirely relative to the position of the observer. Instead, these spirals of Universal Life-Force Energy should be seen as nothing more than energy that is flowing through an alpha-omega cycle of complementary polarity and expansion/contraction.

What Drunvalo Melchizedek helped me understand is that it is important to work with both spirals in order that we remain in balance. Another important thing that I learned from him is that clockwise energy fields draw energy into the center point of the Vortex/Merkaba, just as the counterclockwise field expands energy out from the center.

I have been working with this concept for some time now and I have come to realize that the clockwise field is the lowering of Universal Life Force Energies into physical manifestation, and that the counterclockwise field is the expansion of these energies and the raising of their vibration. We can therefore think of the clockwise field as that which draws in Universal Life Force Energies which cleanse and purify our bodies, and the counterclockwise field as that which expands and raises our vibrations.

In preparation for your Merkaba initiation I suggest that during your daily meditations you experiment with both the clockwise and counterclockwise fields. First, I suggest that you use the clockwise field to ground Universal Life Force Energies into your body. Then experiment with using the counterclockwise flow to raise your vibrations and expand your energy field.

In group ceremonies the clockwise field is used to ground Universal Life Force Energies into the Earth. The counterclockwise field is then used to expand the energies and prayers over the Earth. Both fields can be used at once if the group is very harmonious and serious about this work, but it should be realized that the average group will not be ready to go deeply into using both spirals simultaneously until the latter part of the 1990s.

Merkaba technology is the mastery of counter-rotating fields of energy for reality creation. The profound significance of the reality-creating abilities of counter-rotating energy fields can be illustrated by observing the counter-rotating structures of the classic DNA molecule, galactic spirals, and the Eyes of God.

MER = Light, KA = Spirit, BA = Physical body

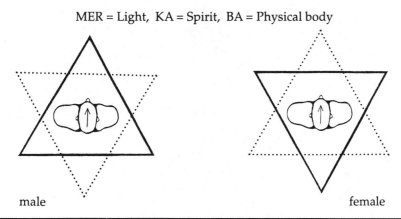

male   female

Meditate on the reality of the star tetrahedron energy field that surrounds your body. This does not mean to *visualize* an energy field; instead, you must live it by allowing yourself to actually experience it.

THE MIRROR–TWIN SPIRALS OF DNA ARE MANIFESTATIONS OF UNIVERSAL VORTEX ENERGY

DNA is a profound example of universal Vortex/Merkaba energy patternings. It is with DNA that the I AM presence manifests consciousness on the third-dimensional plane. As our bodies change into Christ Consciousness vehicles we can expect our DNA to take on new codings that will allow our physical bodies to access spiritual forces we currently know very little about.

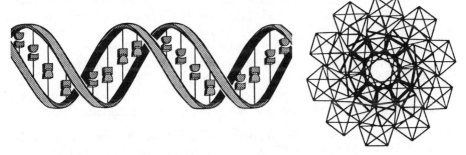

The two primary spirals of DNA are mirror images of one another. On the left is a simplified diagram that does not illustrate the complexity of the geometries formed by DNA's chemical bonds. These bonds are better illustrated by the graphic on the right. DNA is composed of *ratcheted dodecahedrons* that are rotated in increments of 36 degrees, thus having **ten segments** per complete rotation.

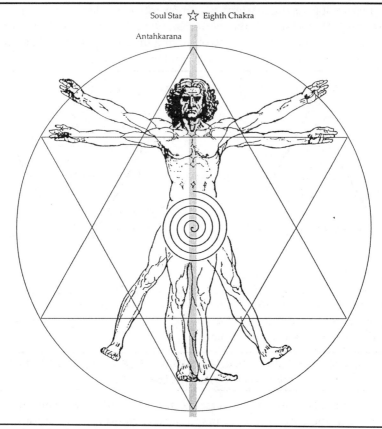

Soul Star ☆ Eighth Chakra

Antahkarana

The two interlocking triangles represent the three-dimensional tetrahedrons of the star tetrahedrons of the Merkaba field.

One of the interesting synchronicities involved in my discovery of Drunvalo Melchizedek's teachings is that during my meditations on what type of material to include in the Ascension yoga section of this book, I often pulled in the mental image of a famous drawing by Leonardo DaVinci, *Canon of Proportions.* I felt that this image could be used to help illustrate what *The Keys of Enoch* refers to as the "interlocking Light pyramids" of the eighth and ninth chakras. Imagine my pleasant surprise to find that Drunvalo Melchizedek refers to this image throughout his lectures as an important illustration of the geometries of the Merkaba.

The triangles are not part of the original drawing; instead, they are implied by the various vertical and horizontal lines Leonardo superimposed on and about the human figure. The ratio of these lines also conforms to what Kabbalists refer to as the "natural array" of the Tree of Life. I have altered the geometry of the original drawing by placing a symmetrical Star of David in the circle and moving the circle down so that *its center now occupies the same position as the figure's base chakra.* In this position the design falls into an interesting symmetry in which the arms are bisected by the base of the downward-facing triangle.

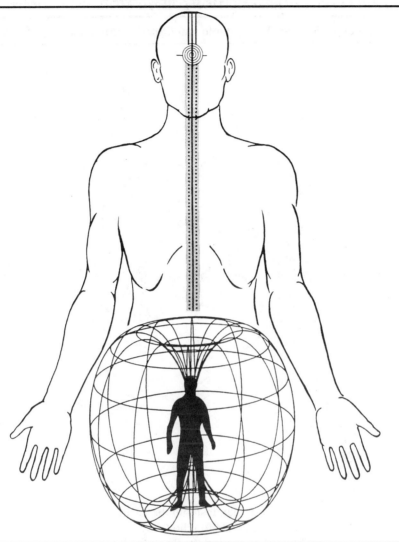

To prepare for the Merkaba initiation, practice becoming aware of a two-way energy flow in the Antahkarana. With the breath, draw Prana in through the top of the head/crown chakra, while you simultaneously draw Shakti Kundalini from the Earth, up through the perineum. Combine these energies in the heart, then radiate the energy throughout your body and your auric field. As you do this you may repeat the following mantra to help you in the creation of a Merkaba field that both transforms and protects.

I accept the blessings of the Infinite Spirit in all things,
I am an immortal, indestructible diamond.

Spiraling energy fields are brought into manifestation through an act of *Will*.

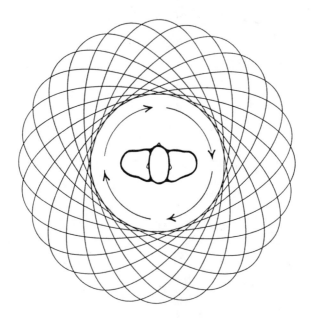

I am soul manifest into the Earth,
I understand who I am,
I am blessed by the Infinite Spirit in all things
I cleanse myself, I heal myself, I purify myself.

ALOHA

As we perfect our Merkabas and build energy in our Light Body, one of the natural results will be that these energies will burn impurities out of our physical and spiritual bodies.

The words visualization, intention and Will all describe the same metaphysical principle: the ability that each human has to call things into manifestation, or to "magnetize" things to oneself with a mental command as an act of Will. We have the ability to do so because each human is an aspect of the Universal Mind, which is limitless and all-powerful.

As we perfect our Merkabas, and build up energy in our systems, one of the natural results will be that these energies will burn out impurities that exist in our physical and spiritual bodies. As part of this process, memories that are stored in our mental bodies and in various parts of our physical bodies (such as the bones, muscles, and various organs) will be triggered as the energy moves through that area. This is one of the reasons why people who meditate often find themselves remembering events they had not thought of in years, that may, or may not seem to have any real significance.

As part of the process of becoming a clear channel for Universal Life-Force Energies, it is important to clear all these memories as they come up. One way to do this is to be alert during your meditations for moments when *pictures* come into your mind. When they do, you are advised to not give them any thought: do not try to rewrite them, or indulge in any "could haves" or "should haves." Instead, you are advised to use your mind's eye to see a tiny point of light in the distance to which you project these random memories as they come up. If you do not dispose of these random memories in this manner, and start thinking about them instead, you will reintegrate them into your energy system.

In human beings the powers of manifestation and magnetization are activated by merely thinking about something happening, or seeing it in the mind's eye. This is why we must learn to think positive thoughts at all times. In fact, our positive evolution is dependent upon clearing our minds of undesirable and destructive thoughtforms, because these thoughtforms have the ability to cause damage to the individual thinking them, to the environment and to other people.

There are two reasons why ascension into the realms of existence where thoughts instantly manifest cannot take place until the individual human is "clear." One is that disharmonious thoughtforms create distortions in individual human energy fields that block out the higher vibrations of the Christ Consciousness energies; and, secondly because in the realms of instant thought/action, stray thoughts can blow a human away instantly.

As for how the individual can attain the desired state of mental clarity and harmony, the first stage must be to simply be aware of the type of internal dialogue one is using and then work to keep this self-imaging positive. This technique should include prayer – **asking the God within us and the Master Christ to help in clearing the mental body of disharmonious energies.**

Advanced techniques for becoming mentally clear include doing various meditations such as the Merkaba and Pillar of Light. These techniques increase the energy level and vibration of the physical, mental, and emotional bodies. When the more refined energies of Christ Consciousness/Love are accessed, they help us to clear undesirable and disharmonious energies from our bodies, thus helping us attain the desired state. Training people to do this is one of my specialties, so think about making it to Sedona for a Soul Star attunement. I can be contacted through the address in the front of this book.

The ten-sided regular polygon, or "decagon," can be considered to be two pentagons that overlap one another 36 degrees apart. This figure was used as the basic design for Gothic cathedrals. It contains ten inner spokes radiating from the center at 36 degrees (1/4 of the light harmonic fractal 144). I see this as one of the best arrangements for the group Merkaba for several reasons:

1. The ten positions relate to the Ten Sephiroth, or primary energies of the Infinite Light (Ain Soph) that emanate from the Godhead. The Ten Sephiroth are the Light/energy patterns that create the Tree of Life, which connects all life systems in all universes and dimensions. The Sephiroth have a direct relation to the formation of the numbers 1,2,3,4,5,6,7,8,9 and 10.

2. Each complete rotation of DNA has 10 segments separated by the same angles as the decagon.

3. *The Keys of Enoch* clearly states that groups of ten people working together as a "family" can call in a Merkaba that will be piloted by three Angelic entities. This will then establish a light communication between realms that will result in the family being transported into a higher realm of light. (Key 305:33)

4. The architects of the Gothic cathedrals were highly educated in the esoteric aspects of Christ Consciousness and sacred geometry. It seems, therefore, wise to use the energy patterns that they chose for their own ceremonial structures.

5. The twelve major programming points of the planetary grid are decagons. See point 18, Bermuda Triangle.

As for the ceremonial use of this pattern for the formation of the Merkaba, the various concepts given in the section of this book entitled "Ascension Yoga" should be the basic guideline. Always remember to begin with a prayer, asking that the Master Christ be with the group and act as a guide. It is also important to invite Angels, who are in service to the Master Christ and positive human evolution, into the circle to act as guides.

Sound is a very important tool that should be used in these ceremonies. The *Keys of Enoch* clearly states that the sacred mantra, Kodoish, Kodoish, Kodoish Adonai 'Tsebayoth should be used. I also feel very strongly about the benefits of using the **Aloha** sound vibration. And calling in the Angels that form the collective Pillar of Light: Michael, Gabriel, Raphael, Uriel

When these names are used and directed toward the center of the circle, the sound vibration helps create a powerful Pillar of Light that will assist in calling in the Angelic Merkaba which is to appear overhead. (See Keys 116, 205, 301, and 305:36)

Method A: BASIC

Have the ten participants move into a circle,
standing at arm's length from one another.

Method B: PRECISE

Mark a spot that will become the center of the circle. Holding a string or rope at this point, use it to scribe the circumference of the circle. It will be helpful to use a piece of rope that has a known length. Twelve feet of rope (144 inches) will make a 24-foot circle. This will result in each person having 45 inches of space.

Method C: EASY

Mark a 24-foot circle, have the participants find their spots.

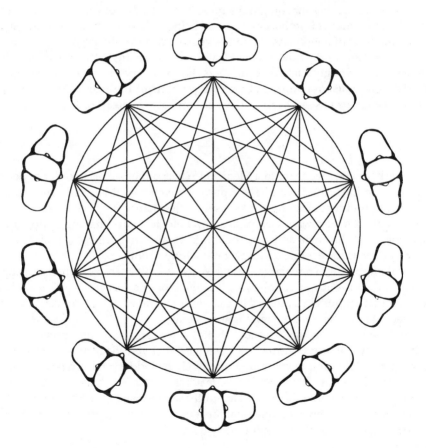

PLANNING FOR CEREMONY

The Keys of Enoch tell us that it is very important for Light workers to use the Vortex/Merkaba/Medicine Wheel technology to anchor the Christ Consciousness program into the heart of the planet by creating pillars of Light in the centers of our Wheels and then using these energy channels to send healing Love energy into the heart of the planet and into the planetary grid.

The Medicine Wheel is Vortex technology. The Medicine Wheel becomes a Merkaba when the energy is applied in the manner described in this book, using prayer, invocation, and the power of creative visualization. Please remember that we are all in the process of learning and there is room for improvisation.

I am particularly interested in working with sound, as I have seen and felt the results of the use of sound. But as to exactly which sounds each group uses, I have only a few suggestions, which will be found in the section of this book devoted to sound. (Intoning *aloha* is one of my favorites.)

Please remember that all groups must have a leader, or anarchy results, but if you are the leader, it is important to avoid being rigid or controlling, as this would block the flow of energy. As stated above, we are all in the process of learning. I cannot tell you exactly how to ascend; all I can do is point in that direction. What I do feel very strongly compelled to say is that **it is very important to activate the Christ Consciousness program by creating pillars of Light and then using these energy channels to send healing Love energy into the heart of the planet.**

It is not necessary to build a Medicine Wheel out of stones in order to perform these ceremonies, but if you have a private area where it is appropriate to do so you might find that building a Wheel seems to enhance the positive energy of the space. I am not sure whether this is a psychological effect having to do with the symbology of the circle and cross or if it is because the symbol actually helps to hold and focus the energies. I suspect it is a little of both.

It is important to remember that if a Wheel is built in an area where anyone can have access to it, it can be misused. It is therefore important to disassemble any Wheels that are built in a public place after the ceremony. (Or better yet, build your Wheel out of nothing more than Light and Love.)

As mentioned in the "Author's Note," there are many interpretations as to what quality the directions have, so I suggest that you focus primarily on higher concepts such as simply communing with God, Goddess, the Angels, the Archetypes, the Stars, and Universal Love, leaving the Native American teachings of animal spirits, tobacco offerings, etc., to those who belong to that culture. (Sage smells nice but it is not a requirement for ceremony as the energy fields you will be generating will clear the space infinitely better.)

Within the precise geometries of the planetary grid there is a more subtle, irregular and organic network of energy lines that connect a myriad of individual power spots together. Many of these places are areas of concentrated life: forests, jungles, and cities. Natural geological features, such as rivers, valleys, mountains, mineral deposits, and faults also create natural gathering places and channels for currents of life force to circulate within the grids.

In regard to our work it is important to note that lines of energy within the grid can be worked with, created, or made stronger through prayer, meditation, and ceremony. One of the main purposes of this book is to inspire groups and individuals in as many places as possible to begin consciously projecting Love and Christ Consciousness thought-energy into the grid and the center of the Earth with Pillars of Light.

When we take it upon ourselves to begin working with the Universal Life-Force Energies and the grid we move into a realm that requires not so much analysis as it does instinct and emotion. Working with Universal Life-Force Energy is an intuitive process that is refined through practice and guidance. The study of the geometrics of the UVG grid is important because it demonstrates that there is indeed an underlying intelligence in nature; but ultimately we need to go beyond descriptions and analysis and get into the energies themselves.

SEEKING GUIDANCE FROM THE MASTERS

The spoken word and intention are two of the most powerful tools that we can use to make our ceremonies powerful and effective. Throughout the world, mystic traditions rely on prayer and intention to "qualify" the energy of ceremonies, to invoke guides, and to direct energy. **The ability of prayer to qualify energy is one of the most important concepts to be aware of**. To qualify energy is to ask for what is wanted (or not wanted). Qualifying energy with prayer *programs* the Universal Mind to send you what you ask for.

As an example, if you want to work with Christ energy, and therefore be protected from all things negative and undesirable, ask out loud that the Master Christ be with you and that all other guides and masters that are drawn to you serve the Master Christ, and work for **"positive human evolution, and ever-ex-panding life."**

As another example, let us imagine that you want to work with Universal Life-Force Energies for the healing of the planet, but you do not have much experience doing so. In such a case it is appropriate to ask for guidance.

I ask that the Universal Mind guide me in accessing these energies,
I ask for guidance from the Master Christ,
I offer myself in service to the healing of planet Earth.

Merkaba fields, Pillars of Light and other types of energy fields such as grid connections, can easily be brought into manifestation through an act of intention, *Will*, and visualization. Beginners can start activating their abilities by using the following invocation: **"I activate the circuitry within my mind and my Light Body that controls my ability to work with these forces."**

We can create individual or group Pillars of Light using the powers of intention, *Will* and visualization. In group ceremony the leader can ask in prayer that a Pillar of Light be placed over the group and that each individual in the group receive guidance in accessing these energies and creating the Pillar of Light. Sound, such as the Aloha chant, should be used to *tune up* the Pillar of Light.

After the Pillar of Light has been invoked, the power of *Will* can be used to make this energy expand and grow. As the amount of Universal Life-Force Energies in the energy field builds, it automatically cleanses and purifies the individuals in the ceremony, **particularly if it is invited to do so.** After the participants are cleared, the energy can then be expanded to cleanse and purify the home or ceremonial area, and then further expanded in stages to purify and empower the local community and countryside. **It is also highly recommended** that the Pillar of Light be used to send Universal Life-Force Energies into the center of the Earth.

Some of you who read these words are natural leaders and teachers, so I encourage you to put the concepts in this book to use and organize a group. What I have found over the past few years is that more and more people are becoming open to the possibilities that exist, regardless of the fact they may not have experience or training in working with these energies. It seems quite natural for people to want to come together in prayer and ceremony for the healing of the Earth.

Remember that prayer and intention control these energies: When you send Love energy into the grid **or connect your Wheel to the grid,** you do not have to know what the mechanics are or which route the energy should take. Instead, make a prayer **asking for the desired result** and know that it is being done automatically.

My vision of ascension is a bit different from Drunvalo Melchizedek's as I think that it is quite possible that a large majority of people might not master their individual Merkabas before this planet enters the electromagnetic null zone. Instead, I feel that most people who survive the transition intact will do so as part of a group Merkaba under the guidance of Angels.

The group Merkaba/Medicine Wheel techniques given in this book should be considered to be phase one of what is possible. I have written about the group Merkaba in this book because I have been guided to do so and because I can see that it will be a good thing for people to learn how to get together to bring in the Light. I am also certain that these ceremonies will have a powerful effect on both the participants and the planet. Because of this I encourage you to put the information about the group Merkaba/Medicine Wheel to use, by organizing a Merkaba group in your area.

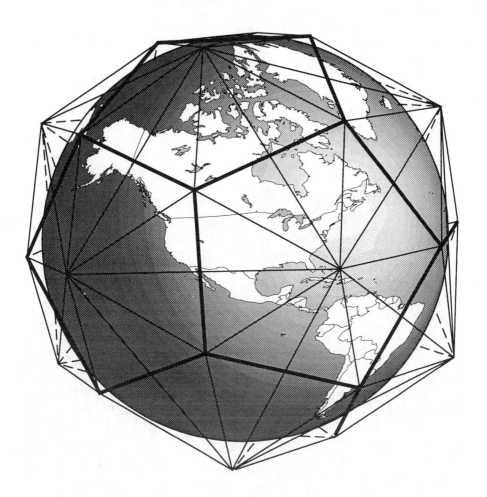

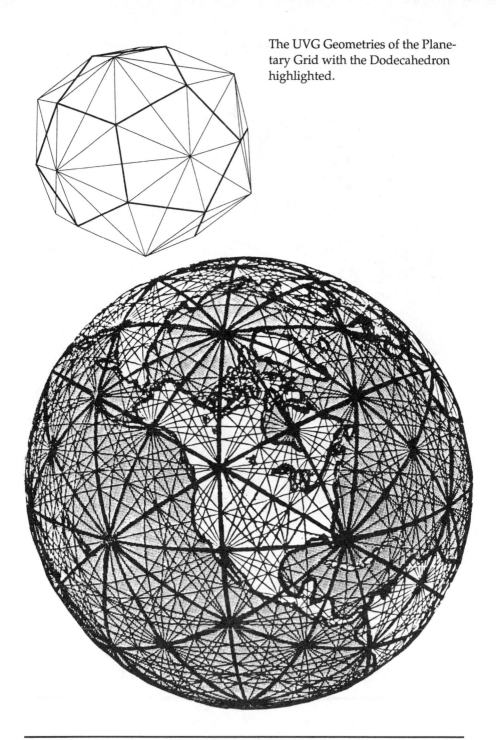

The UVG Geometries of the Planetary Grid with the Dodecahedron highlighted.

The 120 Great Circle Tracks of the UVG

Some of the concepts and words used in this section may be somewhat complex, but if you have the desire to understand the mysteries of creation, I suggest that you read all of this material. If you do not understand some of the terms used, please refer to a dictionary. The letters UVG stand for unified vector geometry. The UVG is the basis of the planetary grid, as proposed by professors William Becker and Bethe Hagens. The word "polyhedron" means "many angles or faces." The Platonic Solids (tetrahedron, octahedron, cube, icosahedron, and dodecahedron) are all polyhedrons.

I think that the most important thing brought to our attention through the study of the planetary grid is that this information demonstrates that all things are part of a grand universal plan that needs to be looked at seriously as a guide for structuring our decisions on managing our world. The number of connections and correspondences between systems – such as geometry, biology, astronomy, etc., that are revealed by this study are immense, as all things are truly interrelated. We can only hope that the people who currently steer our course as a society (the politicians and bankers) begin to wake up to the fact that we "metaphysical people" have access to information that is essential to the continuation of our species.

In presenting this material I owe a debt of gratitude to Professors William Becker and Bethe Hagens and to Governor's State University of Illinois for allowing their research to be shared with the public so freely. Remember to look for Bethe Hagens' book on the planetary grid, which is scheduled to be released sometime soon.

One of the many interesting things that should be noted in our discussion of planetary grid research is that the ancients apparently used a system for understanding the nature of the Earth that is very similar to the UVG system we are currently studying. This amazing revelation comes to us as a result of the research that was originally conducted by Professors Becker and Hagens.

They note that Plato, in his discourse *Timaeus*, alluded to having knowledge of the UVG grid, as he spoke of "the ideal body of the cosmos" being a synthesis of the Platonic Solids (as the UVG is). He also placed an emphasis on the importance of right triangles, such as those which form the UVG, because the faces of all the Platonic Solids can be divided into triangles such as this. Plato saw this particular form of right triangle as a primal component in the formation of all things.

In his discourse *Phaeado*, Plato makes the amazing statement that "the Earth itself looks from above, if you could see it, like those twelve-patched leather balls." This statement appears to indicate that Plato had either astrally projected into a position high above the Earth, and was able to view some of the energy lines of our planet, or that he had received this information from someone who had. (Another possibility might be that the ancients had contact with extraterrestrials.) Whatever the case, a "ball sewn together from twelve patches of leather" apparently describes a dodecahedron, which is considered by many to be the most revered and secret form studied by the ancient geometers. When the dodecahedron is combined with the icosahedron they form the synthesis of all five Platonic Solids which we now refer to as the Unified Vector Geometries.

Two of the most intriguing pieces of evidence to suggest that the ancients had knowledge of the underlying geometrics of our planet are two maps that were introduced to the modern world through the research of professor Charles H. Hapgood in his book *Maps of the Ancient Sea Kings*. These are the di Cantrestis and the Piri Re'is maps, both of which Professor Hapgood discovered in Istanbul, Turkey, in 1929. Both of these maps are centered on the library of Alexandria and use right triangles which correspond to triangles of the UVG grid. The documentation that comes with these maps claims that they were copied from other maps that originally came from the library of Alexandria.

It is interesting to note that the Piri Re'is map, which is attributed to the great admiral of the Turkish/Ottoman navy Piri Re'is, and dated 1513 A.D., was denounced by scholars as being *too accurate to be considered authentic*, for a variety of reasons including the fact that it contains accurate details of the South American coastline as well as details of the Antarctic land mass that were not known to modern science until 1958! This map also contains clear renditions of the Atlantic sea bottom connecting South America to the Antarctic that could only have been visible before, or during the last ice age! (What this hints at is that there was indeed a great prehistory civilization on this planet, such as Atlantis, that had a considerable knowledge of the universe.)

Another interesting thing we can note in our pursuit of ancient connections to this timeless wisdom is that Professor Hagens has discovered that the Sioux Indians have preserved an ancient teaching which states that our planet is somehow bound together, preserved, or created by "16 hoops" that are presumably composed of Universal Life-Force Energy (the Web). The UVG grid is composed of 15 primary great circles which map out the vertices and edges of an icosahedron and dodecahedron that are nested in one another. The addition of the equator gives us a system of *16 great circles!* thus fulfilling the terms of this ancient Native American teaching.

Perhaps at this point we should pause for a moment to speculate on the source of the Sioux people's knowledge of these energies that constitute the basic foundation of our reality.

THAT WHICH IS SACRED IS ABSOLUTE AND IMMOVABLE,
AND THAT WHICH IS ABSOLUTE IS OF GOD.

The study of the planetary grid should be considered an integral part of the study of philosophy and sacred geometry. The planetary grid is a manifestation of the primal energy patternings of the Universal Mind. This is why the grid contains energy patterns which are identical to those we find in the Flower of Life and the sacred geometrics.

In the original Greek, the word "geometry" means "to measure the Earth." The concept of becoming familiar with the Earth in this way is a natural product of our evolution, as this planet is our focal point in the universe, and all things that we observe, whether they be Earthbound or stellar, are judged in relation to the Earth and our bodies, which are of the Earth.

In the western mystic tradition, the origin of the study and use of the planetary grid is attributed to the entity who was known to the Greeks as Hermes and to the Egyptians as Thoth. It is from Hermes that we get the expression "As above, so below," and it is from his Egyptian name Thoth that we get the word "thought." Hermes was an advanced teacher of universal wisdom who evidently belonged to the Order of Melchizedek. According to *The Keys of Enoch*, the Melchizedek Order is a universal order that carries the wisdom teachings of God throughout the universe. The *Keys* also states that the Order of Melchizedek is responsible for erecting pyramidal structures throughout the universe.

On planet Earth, the Melchizedek Order, under the direction of the Master Enoch, erected many of the various pyramids found throughout the world. These pyramids were built as resonators and conductors for both divine and stellar energies. Today these pyramids are found at various places on this planet in a band around the equator that is for the most part within the tropical latitudes of 23.5 degrees north and south.

The secret of the pyramids and their relation to the planetary grid is temporarily lost to us, but modern research has found that many of the well-known megalithic sites coincide with various nodes and lines of known planetary geometrics. It is also interesting to note that Stonehenge and several other megalithic sites in Great Britain can be shown, through geometrics, to have an obvious connection to the grid.

The Keys of Enoch contains quite a bit of material that can be seen to have a relation to this subject. One of the passages in *The Keys* that I find particularly interesting states that the "Priesthood of On" built Stonehenge. (On is known to us now as Heliopolis, the city where Plato and many others studied "The Mysteries.") The *Keys* also tells us that the planetary grid is the result of star energies that form the greater interstellar grid that is an integral part of the universe itself.

Key 105:8+9 clearly states that lines of force from the stars establish a systematic pattern for programming and control of individual species. This same Key, in paragraph 7, also states that the Pleiades are "one of the primary centers" for controlling our planetary grid. (Also see paragraph 11, in relation to grid point 18.)

An interesting confirmation of the profound universal importance of the Unified Vector Geometrics is that science has discovered that the simplest of biological life forms, the virus, is enclosed in a membrane that duplicates the Unified Vector Geometrics! (As above, so below....)

Modern planetary grid research is being carried on by many groups, individuals, and governments. In America the best-known researchers are Professors William Becker and Bethe Hagens, Chris Bird (author of *The Secret Life of Plants)*, and Bruce Cathie (of New Zealand). The research of Becker, Hagens, and Bird was catalyzed by an article that appeared in the official publication of the Russian Academy of Sciences titled "Is the Earth a Large Crystal?"

The authors of this article, Nikolai Goncharov, an historian; Vyacheslav Morozov, an engineer; and Valery Makarov an electronics engineer, had worked together on their theory for several years and had come to the conclusion that our planet has an underlying structure that conforms to the shapes of the icosahedron and dodecahedron nested together.

According to their essay, which appears in David Hatcher Childress' *Anti-Gravity and the World Grid,* Professors Becker and Hagens originally learned about the Russian grid theory in 1983, through an article entitled *Planetary Grid* by Chris Bird, which they found in the May 1975 issue of New Age Journal. Upon reading the article Becker and Hagens noticed that the Russian grid had the basic geometry of a geodesic dome. After consulting *Synergetics II* by Buckminster Fuller (a well-known engineering genius and the inventor of the geodesic dome), Becker and Hagens realized that by connecting the vertices of the icosahedron and dodecahedron in the Russian grid together the resulting shape forms what Mr. Fuller called a rhombic triacontahedron. This form is apparently one of the most important and primal energy patterns in our universe, and the basic energy pattern for all spheres in our universe, including our planet.

The rhombic triacontahedron is the "highest frequency" regular polyhedron, as it is composed of 120* identical right triangles. These triangles are the result of 15 "great circles," each of which divides the sphere into two equal halves, like the equator divides the Earth. During his studies of the sphere Mr. Fuller experimented with balloons and found that when they are inflated to near their limits and then examined closely with the proper optical equipment, their membranes will automatically organize themselves into the great-circle patterns of the rhombic triacontahedron. This indicates that the "theory" of universal energy patterning is more than a theory. It is a fact of nature.

Professors Becker and Hagens took the liberty of adopting a new name for the rhombic triacontahedron, calling it the Unified Vector Geometry, or UVG. All of the maps in this book are based on this form.

Buckminster Fuller was one of the greatest engineers of our time, and he was not the slightest bit bashful about proclaiming that his research indicated that all phenomena in our universe have a metaphysical basis. In fact, his writing indicates that he was keenly aware of the existence of the Universal Mind.

---

* Please note that 120 squared is 14,400 – a fractal of 144,000

The contemplation of the planetary grid is one of the highest forms of philosophical research because it relates to all sciences, including physics, astronomy, chemistry, biology, genetics, meteorology, geology, anthropology, mathematics, and geometry. (Did I leave anything out?)

To simplify our discussion and to tie all this together without going into hundreds of pages of explanations, I will simply state that the planetary grid is a Merkaba within the greater Merkaba, which is the universe itself. The Merkaba is the intelligence vehicle that carries the primal energy patterns that create our universe. Nothing in this universe comes into manifestation without the energy codings of the Universal Mind that are carried throughout the universe by the Merkaba. Each individual human also has a Merkaba, that is a reflection of the universal energy patterns.

The UVG grid is the realization of the concepts put forth by the ancient philosophers, as it is the composite of all five Platonic Solids, which are known to be the basis for all other forms. The Unified Vector Geometrics should be understood to be the synthesis of the Platonic Solids.

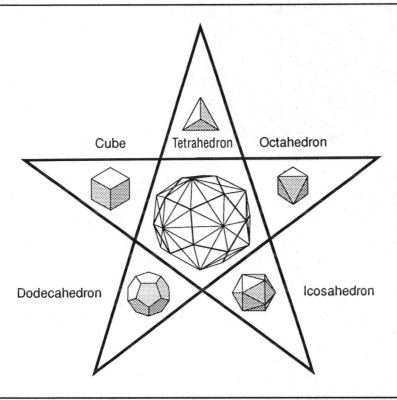

The first spherical polyhedron; the icosahedron stands out as the basic element of the Unified Vector Geometrics. The icosahedron is associated with the element water, which is the Universal Mana of Life. In metaphysical terms, space is "water." (See Key 105:6)

THE GEOMETRIES OF THE PLANETARY GRID
ARE AN ASPECT OF THE UNIVERSAL MERKABA

Key 301:13 of the *Keys of Enoch* tells us that the Merkaba, in its highest sense, is a direct connection to the Mind of God, and that all the energy patternings that create our universe (sacred geometry/universal geometrics) are controlled by the Merkaba. All individual units within the universe such as electrons, humans, planets, stars, galaxies, and supergalaxies, have their own Merkaba fields, which are an aspect of the greater Merkaba of the universe. This is one way we can understand what Einstein was referring to when he spoke of the "unified field." It is this unified field that carries the energy patternings of the Universal Mind throughout the universe.

The Secondary Great Circle Tracks of the UVG Create "the Web"

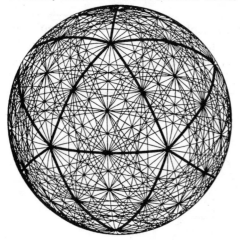

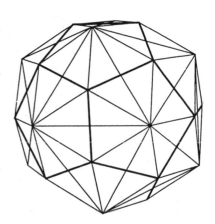

The web pictured in this illustration is created by *secondary* great circles that pass through all the vertices of the original 120 UVG triangles.

The Secondary Great Circle Tracks of the UVG Create "the Web"

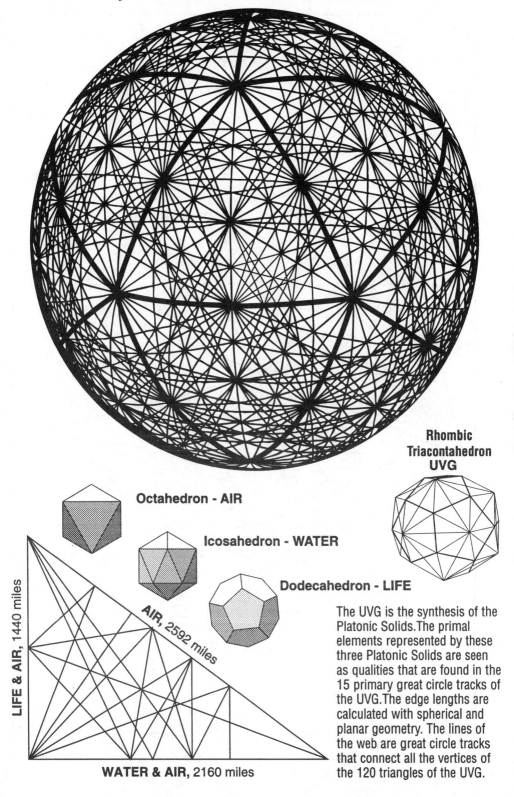

Rhombic Triacontahedron UVG

Octahedron - AIR

Icosahedron - WATER

Dodecahedron - LIFE

LIFE & AIR, 1440 miles

AIR, 2592 miles

WATER & AIR, 2160 miles

The UVG is the synthesis of the Platonic Solids. The primal elements represented by these three Platonic Solids are seen as qualities that are found in the 15 primary great circle tracks of the UVG. The edge lengths are calculated with spherical and planar geometry. The lines of the web are great circle tracks that connect all the vertices of the 120 triangles of the UVG.

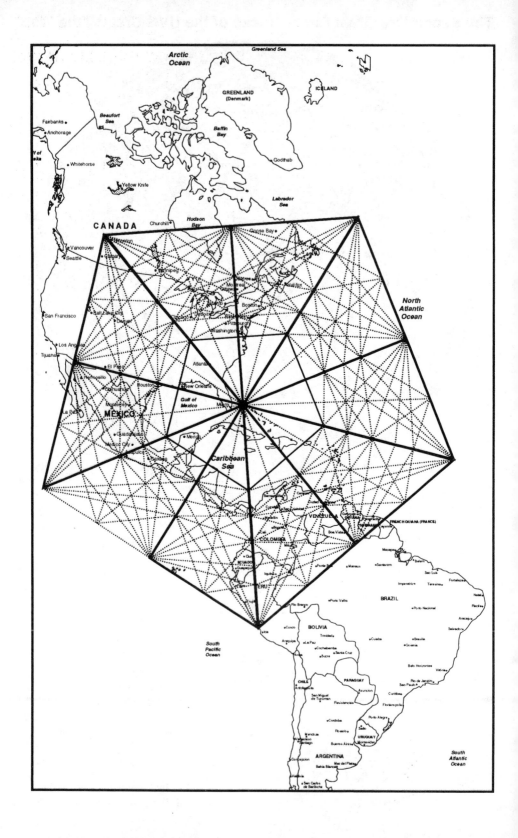

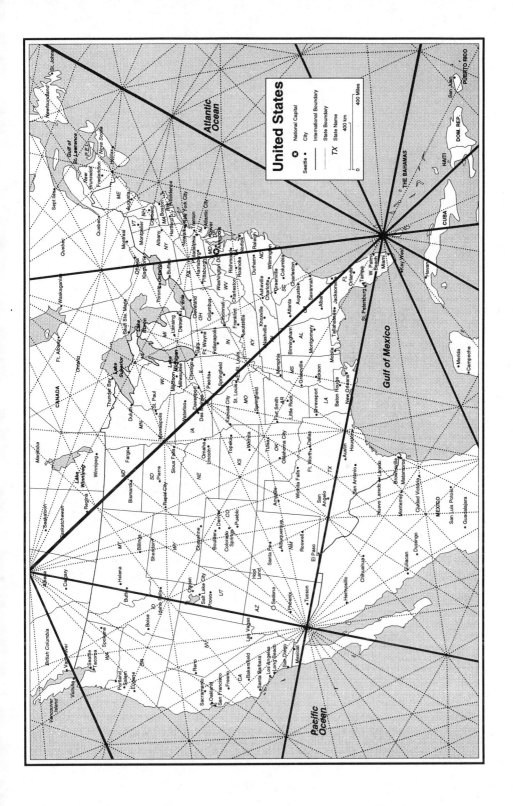

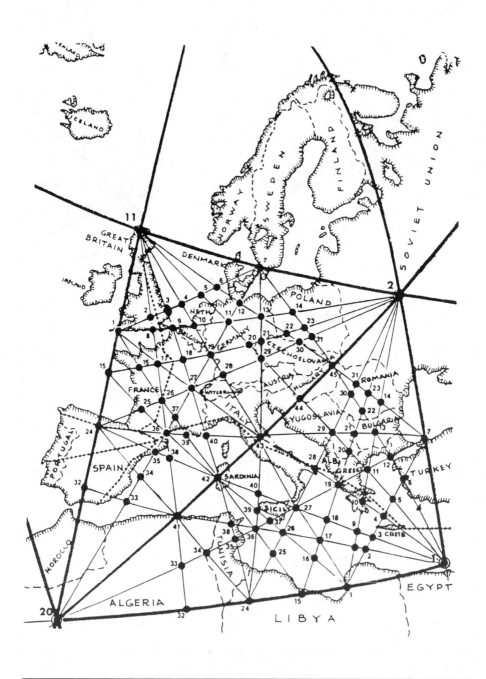

Map of Europe by William Becker and Bethe Hagens

This three-dimensional "Earthstar Map" is based on the UVG geometries. It is available from Adventures Unlimited (815-253-6390) for approximately $15. It comes as a flat piece of paper that can be easily assembled into a three-dimensional globe with pedestal.

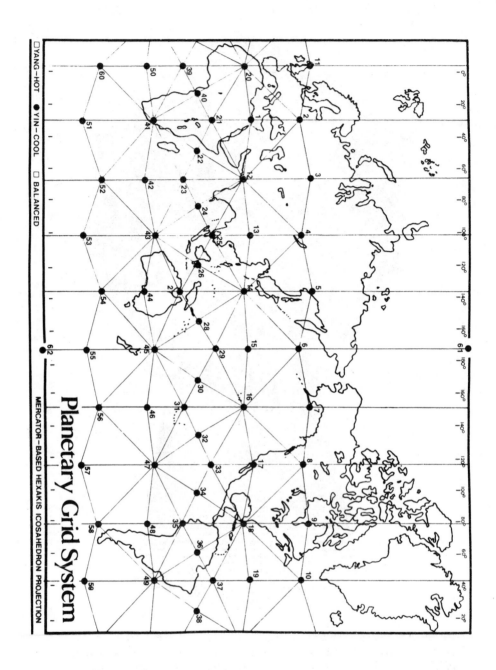

Planetary Grid System

MERCATOR-BASED HEXAKIS ICOSAHEDRON PROJECTION

□ YANG—HOT

● YIN—COOL

□ BALANCED

POINTS ON THE PLANETARY GRID

The descriptions of these points are taken from an essay by William Becker and Bethe Hagens entitled *The Rings of Gaia*, which appeared in *The Power of Place*, and from a magazine article by Becker and Hagens entitled "The Planetary Grid: A New Synthesis" which originally appeared in the *Journal of SITU*, and was later reprinted in David Hatcher Childress' *Anti Gravity and the World Grid*. I have expanded on some of the references, particularly in regard to Points 1 and 17. I will once again thank Professor Hagens for allowing me to use this material and acknowledge Christopher Bird for his original research and profound insight into the nature of reality.

1. 31.72N 31.20E: On the Egyptian continental shelf on the Mediterranean Sea, at approximately the midpoint between the two outlets of the Nile at Masabb Rashid and Masabb Dumyat. The Great Pyramid at Giza is located about 70 miles south and five miles east of this point.

This point appears to be a logical orientation point for a variety of reasons, including the fact that nodes naturally occur in the UVG at 31.72N. This point is also about 40 miles east of the site of the Library of Alexandria, which in ancient times was the central point for the mapping systems discussed earlier in this section. It is interesting to note that the ancient maps were oriented very closely to this point, as it provides excellent positioning for the other points around the globe.

The north-south meridian that goes through point 1 has been recognized since ancient times as the meridian that passes through the largest area of dry land. Point 1 is also precisely 2160 miles from the equator; 2160 miles is also the diameter of the Moon and the length of the long side of a UVG grid triangle. Another interesting thing about point 1 is that it is approximately in the center of all our planet's landmasses. While this may seem interesting enough in itself, we can also theorize that approximately 240 million years ago, before the continents drifted apart, this area was also in the center of the primordial continent. This is apparently why *The Keys of Enoch* refers to the Great Pyramid as "the White Throne in the Center of the World."

Archaeological points of interest located near Point 1 include the library of Alexandria, the Great Pyramid at Giza, King Herod's fortified palace, the Dome of The Rock, the Temple of Solomon at Jerusalem, and Heliopolis. It is interesting to note that this area was one of the focal points of western culture for thousands of years, and that many of the great teachers and philosophers of the past studied or lived in this area.

2. 52.62N 31.20E: Near Kiev, one of the most beloved cities of the Ukraine, this area is one of the most notable centers of commerce, farming, and mining in eastern Europe.

3. 58.62N 67.20E: Near Tobolsk in Russia.

4. 52.62N 103.20E: Near Lake Baikal, which is thought to be the oldest, deepest, and largest lake on our planet. This lake accounts for approximately one fifth of this planet's fresh water resource.

5. 58.28N 139.20E: In the highlands along the coast of the Sea of Okhotsk.

6. 52.62N 175.20E: A notable United States military base exists near here at the island of Attu in the Aleutians. This area flourishes with marine life.

7. 58.28N 148.80W: Edge of continental shelf in Alaska. The line connecting this area to Point 6 coincides with a unique volcanic zone, that is roughly parallel to the Bering Straits. The massive Prudhoe Bay oil deposits are north of this point, on its northern line.

8. 52.62N 112.80W Buffalo Lake, Alberta. This is the first major intersection north of Sedona and Point 17. This is the area of Canada's most prolific oil and gas reserves as well as its most prolific wheat-farming area. **This area is noted for its approximately 5,000-year-old Medicine Wheel, near Majorville.**

9. 58.28N 76.80E: Just east of port Harrison on Hudson Bay.

10. 52.62N 40.80W: Gibbs Fracture Zone. Along with points 19, 37, 38, 39, 50, and 60 the lands between these points roughly map out the mid-Atlantic fracture zone. This one of the "hot spots" on the ocean floor where molten material from the inner Earth is exuded. Some of the most unique forms of marine life live in areas such as this.

11. 58.28N 4.80W: Loch More, on the west coast of Scotland. Powerful psychedelic mushrooms grow in this area. The secondary Great Circle lines that pass through this area have a direct connection to Point 1 as well as many other notable sites in Europe.

12. 26.57N 76.20E: Bordering the Indus River Valley, this is the area where the Hindu civilization began.

13. 31.72N 103.20E: A major center of the Chinese civilization for at least 3000 years. Just north of this point, on a Great Circle track that connects this point with Point 4, are the Chinese pyramids of Xien, *which are almost exactly on the opposite side of the Earth from Sedona.* This Great Circle also passes through

Washington D.C. and the Bermuda Triangle. For more information on these pyramids see Bruce Cathie's *Bridge to Infinity.*

14. 26.57N 139.20E: Near Japan, in the Pacific Ocean at the intersection of the Kydshu Palau Ridge, the west Mariana Ridge, and the Iwo Jima Ridge.

15. 31.72N 175.20E: At the intersection of the Hess plateau, the Hawaiian Ridge, and the Emperor Seamounts.

16. 26.57N 148.80W: Northeast of Hawaii, midway between the Murray and the Molakai fracture zones.

17. 31.72N 112.80W: Near Sonointa, Mexico, south of Ajo, Arizona, and the Organ Pipe National Monument. **This point is approximately 250 miles southwest of Sedona.** The Organ Pipe area has long been regarded as a place of mystery similar to Sedona. As a word of warning I will mention that this area, and the National Monument in particular, are considered dangerous areas because of the large amount of drugs and illegal immigration coming across the border. So if you go there, camp only in regular campgrounds. This is still the wild west, and many locals carry guns for insurance. The last time Professor Hagens was down there she noticed that there is a large installation of about 50 dish antennas in this area. This may indicate that the government utilizes this area because it has desirable electromagnetic qualities.

I find this to be a very interesting site, not only because it the major grid intersection closest to Sedona, but also because its northern Great Circle track passes close to Prescott, Arizona, where one of the most notable local variations in the Earth's geomagnetic field occurs. **This line also passes through the Great Salt Lake in Utah, which** *The Keys of Enoch* **names as a contact area for the Brotherhood of Light. There is a significant junction of secondary Great Circle tracks in the Salt Lake near Ogden.** This Great Circle track is also of particular interest because it connects with Point 12 (the Indus river valley where the Hindu civilization began) and Point 8, in Canada, which has near it an approximately 5000 year-old Medicine Wheel-type structure that is sometimes referred to as the American Stonehenge. Point 17 is also on the same latitude as Point 18 in the Bermuda Triangle, Point #1, and Point #12 (see previous paragraph).

18. 26.57N 76.80W: The Bermuda Triangle, at the edge of the continental shelf near Great Abaco Island. This north-south Great Circle track passes through **Washington D.C.** and the area of the pyramids in China (see Point #13). Point 18 has direct connections to Points 8 + 35.

19. 31.72N 40.80W: Atlantis Fracture Zone.

20. 26.57N 4.80W: In El Eglab, a highland area at the edge of the Sahara Desert sand dunes.

21. 10.81N 31.20E: Sudan highlands.

22. 0N 49.2E: Somali abyssal plain.

23. 10.81S 67.20E: Vema Trench in the Indian Ocean, at the intersection of the Mascarene Ridge, the Carlsburg Ridge, and the Maldive Ridge into the mid-Atlantic Ridge.

24. 0 85.2E: Ceylon abyssal plain.

25. 10.81N 103.20E: Kompong Som, a natural bay on the southern coast of Cambodia southwest of Phnom Penh. This site is near Angkor Wat, which is an ancient megalithic city that was abandoned in much the same manner as the cities of the ancient Mayans. This north-south Great Circle track passes through Thailand, Laos, Vietnam, and Washington D.C.

26. 0 121.20E: At the midpoint between Teluk and Tomini, a bay in northern Sulawesi.

27. 10.81S 139.2E: Midpoint of the mouth of the Gulf of Carpentaria.

28. 0 157.20E: Center of the Solomon Plateau.

29. 10.81N 175.20E: Midpoint of abyssal plain between Marshall Islands, mid-Pacific mountains, and the Magellan Plateau.

30. 0 166.80W: Nova Canton Trough.

31. 10.81N 112.80W: Society Islands.

32. 0 130.80W: Galapagos Fracture Zone.

33. 10.81S 76.80W: End of the Clipperton Fracture Zone.

34. 0N 94.80W: Junction of the Cocos Ridge and the Carnegie Ridge just west of the Galapagos Islands.

35. 10.81S 76.90W: Lake Punrrun in the Peruvian coastal highlands, the headlands of the Amazon River. This point is near the Nazca Plains and an "enormous pyramid complex" which was described in the April 30, 1990, *U.S. News and World Report.* This area is close to Machu Picchu and major centers of cocaine production.

36. 0 58.80W: State of Amazonas.

37. 10.81N 40.80W: Vema Fracture Zone.

38. 0 22.80W: Romanche Fracture Zone.

39. 10.81S 4.80W: Edge of mid-Atlantic Ridge in Angola Basin, just southeast of Ascension fracture zone.

40. 0 13.20W: Gabon Highlands at intersection of three national borders.

41. 26.57S 31.20E: L'uyenego on the Utsutu River, Swaziland. Just north of this point is Great Zimbabwe a massive ancient structure that is a focal point for Native African mysticism, sometimes referred to as "Africa's Stonehenge." Near this point is also found what may be the world's oldest iron mine, the Ngwenya mine. The north-south Great Circle track is the same one that passes through Point 1.

42. 31.72S 67.20E: Intersection of mid-Atlantic Ridge with the southwest Indian Ridge.

43. 26.57S 103.20E: Tip of Wallabi Plateau.

44. 31.72S 139.20E: In Australia, in a lowland just east of St. Mary's peak, which is the highest point in the area. Near Spencer Gulf. Geophysists have recorded enormous geoelectric currents in the Earth near here in excess of **a million amps!**

45. 26.57S 175.20E: At the edge of the Hebrides Trench, just southwest of the Fiji Islands.

46. 36.72S 148.80W: Somewhere out in the south Pacific....

47. 26.57S 112.80W: Eastern Island Fracture Zone.

48. 31.72S 76.80W: The Nazca Plate.

49. 26.57S 40.80W: Deep ocean at edge of continental shelf.

50. 31.72S 4.80W: Walvis Ridge.

51. 58.28S 31.20E: Enderby Abyssal Plain.

52. 52.62S 67.20E: Kerguelen Plateau.

53. 58.28S 103.20E: Ocean floor midway between Kerguelen abyssal plain and the Wilkes abyssal plain.

54. 52.62S 139.20E: Kangaroo Fracture Zone.

55. 58.28S 175.2E: Edge of Scott Fracture Zone.

56. 52.62S 148.80W: Unintsev Fracture Zone.

57. 58.28S 112.80W: Eltanin Fracture Zone.

58. 52.62S 76.80W: South America at its tip.

59. 58.28S 40.80W: South Sandwich Fracture Zone.

60. 52.62S 4.80W: Bovet Fracture Zone.

61. North Pole.

62. South Pole.

See page 83 for information about this picture.

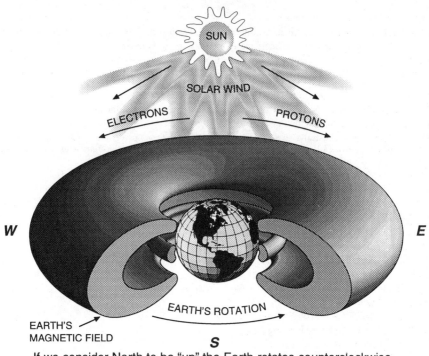

If we consider North to be "up" the Earth rotates counterclockwise.

Star Tetrahedron Merkaba Field In Planetary Sphere

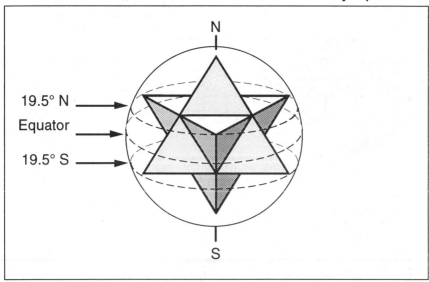

See Richard Hoagland's Video - *Hoagland's Mars II, the UN Briefing* for an excellent explanation of how planetary Merkaba fields work.
Order from Adventures Unlimited (815) 253-6390.

In the study of sacred geometry and the Flower of Life we find that the star tetrahedron is formed within all the Platonic Solids as a *virtual object* that exists but can not be seen. (See illustration: Platonic Solids in Metatron's Cube.) Because of this, metaphysical philosophers often say that the star tetrahedron provides the *seed* that *generates* the Platonic Solids.

Richard Hoagland, a former science writer for NASA, who is best known for the books and videos he has produced about the face on Mars, has found an extremely interesting correlation between the virtual star tetrahedron that exists within the Platonic Solids and significant areas of "major energy upwellings" that exist on the Sun, the Earth, and various other planets in our solar system at approximately 19.5 degrees north or south.

What is particularly interesting about these areas, in relation to our study of Universal Merkaba formation, is that 19.5 degrees north and south are the latitudes where the apex points of a virtual star tetrahedron within any size sphere will contact that sphere's surface! This apparently indicates that these energy up-wellings have a correlation to the star tetrahedron, which, in turn, confirms information given in the *Keys of Enoch* about the Merkaba as the vehicle for the primal forces of creation. (See Richard Hoagland's *Monuments of Mars*, chapter 11.)

HOT SPOTS AT 19.5 DEGREES NORTH AND SOUTH

1. On the Sun: sunspot activity and the region of peak temperature is limited to 19.5 degrees north and south.

2. On Venus: the presumably active major volcanic complexes Alpha and Beta Regio are near 19.5 degrees.

3. On Earth: the largest shield cone volcano is at 19.6 degrees north. This is the Mauna-Kea volcano on the island of Hawaii. The temples of the Sun and Moon in Teotihuacan, Mexico are also at this latitude.

4. On Mars: the "vast" Olympus Mons shield cone volcano is at 19.5 degrees north.

5. On Jupiter: the "red spot," which is an obvious Vortex is at 19.5 degrees.

6. On Neptune: in 1986 Voyager II discovered a similar spot at 19.5 degrees north. The Hubble space telescope has recently discovered that this spot has apparently disappeared. This may or may not mean that the energy that created this Vortex is gone, as it may have simply cycled through to a color that is harder to detect from the vast distance that separates Earth from Neptune.

Richard Hoagland notes that Jupiter, Saturn, and Uranus all radiate more energy than they receive from the Sun, thus indicating that they have "some sort of internal energy source." I will suggest that when the human race learns the secret of this energy source, the results will be far more profound than Mr. Hoagland imagines, and this will result in the human race's transmigration into a realm where thought manifests as energy that instantaneously affects reality.

As for the theory that the star tetrahedron/Merkaba is responsible for the generation of energy within planets, it is interesting to note that one of the most cherished and unscientific beliefs of Earth science is that the electromagnetic field of our planet is generated by "dynamo action" of molten iron in the Earth's core.

The problem with this theory is that it violates a known scientific constant, the Curie point. According to the physics book on my shelf, the Curie point of iron is 1400 degrees. At this point iron ceases to be magnetic. Molten iron exists at about

2000 degrees, and is nonmagnetic because its temperature is above the Curie point. Earth science makes an extremely long stretch of "logic" in maintaining that while they know that molten iron exceeds the Curie point, "dynamo activity" (circular motion) of the molten iron in our planet's core must generate an electrical current that in turn creates the Earth's magnetic field.

Could it be that the Earth's electromagnetic field is the result of Merkaba activity?

An important example of Universal Merkaba formation that we should take note of is the fact that our planet is known to have an exceedingly high-energy counterotating field in the upper level of the ionosphere, where electrons and protons captured from the solar wind travel in opposite directions. (The electrons move from west to east in a counterclockwise direction as the protons move from east to west in a clockwise direction.)

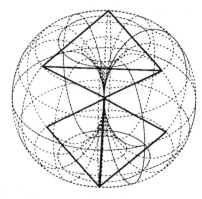

THE TORUS

The torus is one of the primary energy patterns of our universe, and there is a great deal of scientific information available to indicate that the torus is the best model we have for attempting to understand the primal form of the universe, in fact, some physicists have speculated that the universe may be toroidal. The standard joke about this is that because the universe is shaped like a bagel – it must be a sure sign God is Jewish....

The central portion of the torus contains two "conic sections," which, in a manner of speaking, are rotated tetrahedrons (tetrahedrons moving in time). Each tetrahedron has four vertices, thus the two tetrahedrons in a torus have a total of eight vertices. The hourglass-shaped figure created by the two tetrahedrons forms an angular version of the number 8, which, when turned on its side forms the symbol of infinity.

The Keys of Enoch tells us that light cones, or rotating tetrahedral/pyramids, are essential for carrying the "divine programming" of the worlds of manifest creation.

The center of each torus is a Vortex, therefore, the torus should be considered an essential element in universal Vortex formation.

Rotation is one of the primal universal qualities of Universal Merkaba Formation. And it should be noted that rotation is a universal constant. (See Arthur Young, *Reflexive Universe*).

Because all the observable universe is moving through space/time, rotating objects never complete a rotation in exactly the same space where the rotation cycle began. This creates the effect of all known objects spiraling through space.

The spiraling energy pattern of the Vortex appears to be the primary energy pattern of the universe. In fact, galaxies, stars, planets, people, DNA, atoms, electrons, protons, and neutrons are all based on the spiraling Vortex energy pattern. So to make my point, even at the risk of sounding overly "New Agey," I will state that the universe as we know it is a Vortex. Therefore, if we are to evolve we must learn how to be conscious of what we are: Spiraling Vortices of Life-Force Energy.

DNA is a classic example of the both the spiraling nature of Universal Merkaba formation and the balanced counterotating energy fields that we associate with the Merkaba. DNA is also one of the most interesting examples of the information-carrying properties of the Universal Vortex/Merkaba, as the chemical lattice of DNA apparently acts as an antenna for energies that carry the "light codes" that produce organic life. (Physicist Rupert Sheldrake refers to this energy as the "morphogenetic field.")

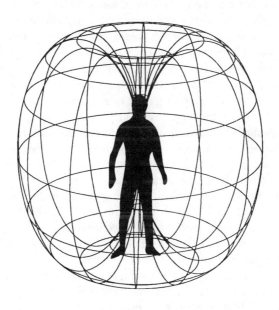

Just as I was completing this book I had a surprise visit from Jose and Lloydine Argüelles that helped draw my attention to some interesting parallels between the Mayan calendar, sacred geometry, and the Flower of Life. These correspondences indicate that we are in the process of discovering some truly profound things about the nature of time and space that promise to revolutionizing the human experience.

As you may remember, Jose Argüelles' book *The Mayan Factor* was *the* catalyst for the Harmonic Convergence in 1987. He was also one of the co-creators of the original Earth Day in 1970. Starting this year, 1995, I think that we can expect to see Jose re-emerge as a leader of the planetary healing movement as he promotes his theory of correct timing as a key to planetary harmony and healing.

I have been interested in Jose Argüelles' work since the time of the Harmonic Convergence, and I consider the success of the Harmonic Convergence to be an indication that his information about the Mayan calendar and universal timing frequencies is correct and *vital to the survival of our species.*

The core of Jose Argüelles' teaching is that our current system of under-standing time – the Gregorian calendar – is not in harmony with the cosmic rhythms that govern our galaxy, and that our use of the Gregorian calendar, which is unnatural and dis-harmonic, creates a situation that results in the human race being out of harmony with the environment. This resultant dis-harmony with the environment has caused humanity to create a system of planetary mismanage-ment that, if not brought under control, will result in a monumental and deadly collapse of our planet's biosphere.

As evidence that this theory is correct, Jose points to the fact that since the time the Gregorian calendar came into use, and particularly since the time of the Industrial Revolution, when all the world began to synchronize with "artificial mechanical time," the population has expanded at an undesirable rate, while the environment has been subjected to an ever-increasing number of short-sighted, profit-motivated attacks of destructive expansion that have led us to our current situation wherein the human population is increasing at an exponential rate while the biosphere teeters on the edge of a wildly catastrophic collapse.

I find Jose's theory of time, harmony and dis-harmony has deep correlation to the age-old dialectic between spirituality and materialism. In "The Prophecy of Pacal Votan," which Jose received while in the Yucatan, we are told that the out-of-control materialism of our current age is the fulfillment of the prophecy of the Beast in the Book of Revelation. As our species gets further and further out of synchronization with galactic timing and the primal forces of creation, we become more and more under the control of the mechanized beast we have created. Jose's vision is that as part of our work as planetary healers, we must become aware of the galactic timing frequency of the Mayan calendar and learn how to use the natural harmonics of time to our advantage. The theory behind this is that when a core group of at least 144,000 becomes attuned to the natural galactic timing frequency, we will find ourselves in control of a vast resource of spiritual energy that can be used to heal the planet.

One of the most interesting aspects of Jose Argüelles' research involves working with what he refers to as galactic gateways. Each unit within the 260 units of the Mayan sacred calendar has a numerical value between 1 and 13, as well as one of 20 qualities or "signs." Jose refers to the number and sign of each of the 260 units in the Mayan sacred calendar as a galactic gateway.

In contemplating the harmonic relationships of the various galactic gateways of this system, it is believed that any date in the Mayan or Gregorian calendar that shares a galactic gateway with another date has a *resonance* with that date. It is therefore extremely interesting to note that the Harmonic Convergence, August 17, 1987, has the **same** galactic gateway as the bombing of Hiroshima!

What this means is that the world peace ceremonies of the Harmonic Convergence occurred on a date that has resonance with what may well have been the most horrific event to have ever occurred on this planet! And, according to the science of Mayan time shamanism, the Love wave created by the ceremonies of the Harmonic Convergence canceled out the nuclear death program that had been initiated by the bombing of Hiroshima.

Part of the magic of this is that at the time of the Harmonic Convergence Jose had not yet discovered the secret of the galactic gateways! This means that the first planetary peace event predicted by the ancient Mayan timekeepers came into existence by the might of its own power *at just the right time* in a 26,000 year cycle, with very little effort or (conscious) planning! Jose and many others see this as a clear indication that higher forces were at work in the timing of the Harmonic Convergence.

A further example of the synchronicities that can occur when one enters into the flow of galactic time is that when Jose originally announced the date of the Harmonic Convergence in his book *The Mayan Factor*, he had no idea that the Sun would be in the **144th degree** of the zodiac that day, or that this event was to be accompanied by a significant planetary alignment of Saturn and Uranus with a point near the galactic center.

Jose's awareness of the August 17, 1987, date began with an obscure reference to this date in the 1971 book *Lord of the Dawn* by Tony Shearer. Tony received this part of the prophecy during the time that he lived and worked in Central America, studying the Mayans and Aztecs. It is doubtful that Tony had any idea that his reference to this date would catalyze a huge planetary event 16 years later.

In retrospect, Jose sees the Harmonic Convergence as a prime example of what he calls "universal telepathy" in action. Only group consciousness could have brought so many people together on a planetary scale for a cosmic event that had no advertising budget or hype. As for those who do not understand the significance of the Harmonic Convergence, or those who say that Jose's interpretation of the Mayan calendar is incorrect, Jose says that the success of the event speaks for itself. Something was obviously happening – why else would people from all parts of the world come together on short notice and "think peace"? After all, which is more powerful: 144,000 people praying for peace – or the atomic bomb?

On July 26, 1992, our planet entered the last 20-year segment of the 26,000-year grand cycle, and the 5200 year great cycle of the Mayan calendar. This last time-space frame of the calendar is governed by its two highest signs: the 13th Ray and the Solar Mind. The date July 26, 1992, shares the same galactic gateway as the test of the first atomic bomb, which was July 16, 1945. Forty-seven years later, groups throughout the world performed world peace ceremonies to cancel the death program of the event that historians refer to as the "Trinity detonation."

The Thirteenth Ray is the highest vibration in the Mayan calendar; it is the ray of transformation. The 20th sign, Solar Mind or "Ahau" reveals the mystery of light, both physical and spiritual. The auspicious combination of these signs indicates that our planet is entering into the time of initiation into the greater Body of Light. This is why Drunvalo Melchizedek's work with the Merkaba has become so popular; the energies of this space/time are becoming naturally conducive for the induction of the human species into the Diamond Vehicle of Light.

As an interesting note in regard to the significance of total solar eclipses it should be noted that in 755 A.D. Mayan priests had predicted that during the eclipse on June 11, 1991, the "masters from the stars" would appear in the valley that later became the home of Mexico City. This prophecy was apparently fulfilled, as several individuals with video cameras recorded what appears to be a flying saucer hovering in the sky below the dark disk of the eclipsed Sun. This appearance has caused quite a stir in Mexico, and videos of this event have been shown on national television there.

You can obtain documentaries of this event through Genesis Video, Box 25962, Munds Park, Arizona, 86017, or these videos can be ordered through your local bookstore. (Distributed by New Leaf.) Ask for: *Masters of the Stars* or *Messengers of Destiny*. Each one is $39.95

HUNAB KU:
ONE GIVER OF
MOVEMENT & MEASURE

If you are interested in learning more about the Mayan calendar and Jose Argüelles' work, please send a stamped, self-addressed envelope to the Vortex Society with a short note asking for information on the Mayan calendar. The address is given in the beginning of this book.

Most of the astronomical information in this section comes from the research of galactic whole-sky astrologer Raymond Mardyks, author of the newly released *Sedona Starseed, a Galactic Initiation*. Please note that this material is written from the perspective of the northern hemisphere. This means that when the northern hemisphere experiences a winter solstice, the southern hemisphere experiences a summer solstice.

In Jose Argüelles' *Dreamspell, Journey of Timeship Earth, 2013*, he suggests that the completion date of the current 5200-year Mayan "great cycle" has a direct correlation to the 26,000-year precession of the equinox, as the number of years in the precession are a "fractal overtone harmonic" of the 260 units that compose the calendar.

In support of this theory Ray Mardyks has determined that a series of notable celestial events that are due to take place between now and 2012 apparently have a direct correlation to the galactic timing frequency of the Mayan calendar, the end of the current 5200-year cycle, and the initiation of our planet into galactic civilization.

There has been a great deal of debate over which day the current cycle ends and the new cycle of galactic consciousness begins, so I think we should take note of what Ray has to say about this, as the celestial clock is always an accurate reflection of galactic time.

While the cycle of the precession of the equinox in itself does not appear to have a clear beginning or end, Ray Mardyks suggests that one of the most important events in the timing frequency of the precession is keyed to the time when the winter and summer solstices achieve exact alignment with the galactic plane. This occurs twice in every 26,000-year cycle and is due to occur again in 1999.

There will also be a total eclipse of the Sun in 1999. In both Mayan and modern astrology, solar eclipses are seen as activation portals for the consciousness programming of our planet. This eclipse will take place on August 11, with totality occurring over eastern Europe at the 11th hour a.m. Greenwich mean time. As this occurs the Sun and Moon will be in the middle of Leo, with Mars, Saturn, and Uranus in the middle of the signs Scorpio, Taurus, and Aquarius, respectively. Astrologers will recognize this configuration as a grand cross. This particular grand cross will form at a point in the heavens that astrologers refer to as "the points of the Avatar." (See illustration of the constellation Aquarius.)

This eclipse is closely linked to another total solar eclipse that will happen November 13, 2012 – 13 years after the 1999 eclipse. This eclipse will be in alignment with the 13th constellation of the zodiac: Ophiuchus the "Serpent Holder." This constellation is the archetype of the shaman/healer that has knowledge of the secret of life. In the terms of galactic whole-sky astrology this eclipse will represent the initiation of our planet into the mysteries that Ophiuchus represents.

From the astrological viewpoint of the science of galactic shamanism, the significance of the winter and summer solstices aligning with the galactic plane is that when this type of alignment occurs it clearly signals the end of one era and the beginning of another.

The scientific/metaphysical explanation for the importance of the solstices as a time of reprogramming and initiation is that at the time of the solstices, large quantities of solar energy enter either the north or south magnetic poles of our planet. This large influx of energy contains an energy/consciousness program from the solar mind that programs the magnetic grid of our planet for the next six-month period.

This energy/consciousness program also carries with it galactic energy from the stars or constellations that the Sun and Earth happen to be in alignment with at that time. In the case of the 1999 winter solstice we find that this event will be in *exact alignment with the galactic plane, in close proximity to the center of the Galaxy and the 13th constellation of the zodiac: Ophiuchus the "Serpent Holder."*

The constellation Ophiuchus represents the galactic energies of the sha-man/healer who has knowledge of the secret of life. In the terms of galactic whole-sky astrology the winter solstice in 1999 will be an initiation of our planet into the mysteries that Ophiuchus represents, and more importantly, an attune-ment to the energies of galactic synchronization that emanate from the Galactic Center.

During the winter solstice of 1999 the south pole of our planet will be directed toward the galactic center as it aligns with the plane of the galaxy and the Sun. At that time the galactic energy/consciousness programs will enter the already exist-ing *hole in the ozone* above Antarctica, and give our planet an initiation of galactic consciousness/energy that is entirely unprecedented in the history of our planet. (Isn't it interesting to imagine that the hole in the ozone may actually be working to our advantage – or, in New Age lingo: opening us up to new energies?)

The 13-year period following the 1999 activation/initiation will be a time of intense change while the human race on planet Earth integrates the new galactic energies that will have been made available to us. The final activations of the series will consist of a series of three astronomical events in quick succession during the year 2012. The first will be the total eclipse on November 13. The second will be the winter solstice, *which is the final solstice in the galactic plane alignment series*. The third event will be December 31, 2012, when Sirius aligns with our planet and the Sun at midnight.

Could one of these celestial events be the end of the 5200-year cycle – Mayan calendar date* 13.0.0.0.0? According to the Gregorian calendar, the end of each year is at midnight, December 31/January 1. But in the system of the Mayans, according to Jose Argüelles, the end of the year is July 25. This discrepancy of the dates for the end of the year has been a stumbling block and a source of confusion for many students of Jose's work, not only because of the fact that July 25 seems to be a strange, if not arbitrary, time to end the year, but also because after the July 26 "Mayan New Year" in 2012, Jose refers to the rest of this year as 2013.

Apparently, the beginning and end of the Mayan year is based on the fact that at the latitudes where the Mayan civilization flourished, the star **Sirius** rises on July 26 shortly before sunrise. What this means, is that *like the Egyptians*, the Mayans began their new year with what is known as the heliacal rising of Sirius. (Helios is the Greek word for the Sun.)

* Ray Mardyks believes that the winter solstice of 2012 is *the date*.

130

This should still leave one wondering why in the world do we not base our Gregorian new year on something logical like the spring equinox or the winter solstice (as our ancestors have done in the past). Ray Mardyks has the answer for this: The beginning of the new year in the Gregorian system is based on the moment in time, each year, when the star *Sirius and the Sun are in opposition to one another, with Sirius at the highest point in the night sky while the Sun is directly on the opposite side of the Earth at midnight on December 31 – in all local time zones.*

What this reveals to us is that there is indeed a certain amount of logic (albeit highly obscured) to the calendrical system that Pope Gregory the 13th imposed on the world. Both systems, Gregorian and Mayan, depend on the star Sirius for their timing, yet these timings represent celestial events that are the opposite of one another. In the Mayan and Egyptian systems the new year begins when the Sun is between Sirius and Earth, whereas in the Gregorian system the year begins when the Earth is between Sirius and the Sun.

What this means to those of us who are interested in working with the galactic timing of the Mayan calendar is that there is a six-month period between the time of the heliacal rising of Sirius and the culmination of Sirius at midnight on December 31 that represents two distinct stages of Earth-Sun-Sirius interactions that should be considered to be significant and inseparable.

It is also interesting to note that in the year 1999 Gregorian, the heliacal rising of Sirius at the latitude of Sedona will occur very close to the date of the August 11 total eclipse. We can also note that the 2012 eclipse occurs 13 years after the 1999 galactic initiation, in the 13th year of the 21st century.

The beginning date of this 5200-year cycle, August 13, 3113 B.C., is based on dates left on stone monuments that the Mayan timekeepers erected in Monte Alban, Mexico. As a harmonic number in the Mayan system, 5200 is seen as the product of 260 x 20. 26,000 can also be divided by 5200 evenly: 26,000/5 = 5200. The number 5,200 is also a harmonic overtone fractal of 52, which is an important number that appears within the 260-unit sacred calendar as 13 groups of four signs whose numerical values add up to 28 (the average length of the lunar cycle.)

A quick check with your calculator will show that 5125 solar years have elapsed since 3113 – not 5200. This is because the years of the Mayan calendar are 360-day cycles that are based on the perfect division of the circle. (There is a difference of 133.8 days between these two time periods.)

An interesting figure comes into play when we multiply the 5200 years by 360 days: 5200 x 360 = 1,872,000. When this figure is divided by 13 (one of the two primary numbers of the Mayan sacred calendar) we arrive at 144,000, the harmonic of light.

For the more information about Ray Mardyks' galactic whole sky astrology, and a sample copy of his Cosmic Calling Newsletter, send a self-addressed stamped envelope to:

STAR HEART PUBLICATIONS   dept 1
P.O. Box 2841 Sedona, Arizona 86339

Jose Argüelles' research demonstrates that the Mayan calendar is based upon a primal mathematic system that is found throughout nature. A notable example of this is Mayan calendar's relation to the 64 hexagrams of the Chinese system of divination known as the I Ching, which in turn can be demonstrated to have a direct relation to the human genetic code. (See Jose Argüelles' *Earth Ascending*.) Because of this fact we can say that the human body is the biological counterpart of the mathematic code of the Mayan calendar.

The 260-unit grid of the Mayan Calendar is the result of the combination of the numbers 13 and 20. Referring to the section of this book on sacred geometry we can see that Metatron's Cube, which is the basis for the formation of the Platonic Solids, is composed of 13 circles. Another interesting correlation is the fact that 7 circles make up the core of Metatron's Cube, and that 7 *is also the central number within the grid of the Mayan calendar.*

The number 20 is an important number in sacred geometry as it is essential to the formation of the icosahedron, the dodecahedron, the UVG geometries, and all other spheres in the universe.

MAYAN CALENDAR   METATRON'S CUBE

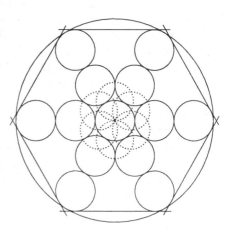

The 20 signs are modified by the 13 powers, creating a matrix of 260 combinations. Dark squares are the 52-unit harmonic matrix that is formed by sets of squares that have a combined value of 28, the average number of days in a lunar cycle.

One does not have to become an expert on these number systems to benefit from them. In fact, the goal is to transcend the linear logic of the numbers as symbols, and merge with the energy that the numbers represent.

Mayan calendar illustration courtesy Jose Argüelles; see his book *Mayan Factor* for more information.

Using traditional astronomical boundaries, the Sun's alignment in right ascension with the constellation Aquarius at the spring equinox is not due to occur until 2050, and the first star in the Aquarius constellation will not to be encountered in this manner until the year 2168. There is, however, another way of looking at this process that sees the first glimmerings of Aquarius appearing during the spring equinox of the year 2000. At this time the Sun's position on the celestial equator will begin to align in right ascension with the boundary of the image of Aquarius.

Beginning of constellation
measured in right ascension
along the celestial equator

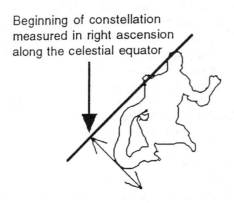

Beginning of constellation
measured in longitude
along the ecliptic/zodiac

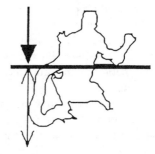

NOTES ON THE THIRTEEN

The number 13 is the most enigmatic of all numbers known to the human race on planet Earth.

The number 13 is a transcendental number in that it represents a quality that is beyond the realm of physicality. This is what makes it one of the primary numbers in the structure of time. Physical reality is based on harmonics of the number three and its first and second harmonics, 6 and 12. In Metatron's Cube we can see how the Platonic Solids are formed by 12 circles around one central circle. This inner circle represents the hidden God-quality within creation.

In the New Testament we find that the Master Christ gathered 12 apostles around him, 12 + 1 = 13.

In the Book of Numbers in the Old Testament we find that there were 13 tribes of Israel, not 12! Most teachers speak of the 12 Tribes of Israel, overlooking the tribe of *Levi*, who, as the guardians of the temple mysteries, were not counted. (This reminds me of how the 13th constellation, Ophiuchus, has traditionally not been counted, in spite of the fact that it represents great knowledge.)

In music, the chromatic scale is composed of 13 notes – 8 whole notes, which are represented by the white keys on the piano, and 5 half-tones, which are represented by the black keys.

The Great Seal of the United States of America, which proudly declares the advent of the new age Novus Ordo Seclorium (a New Order of the Ages) is based on the numbers 13 and 52. The two sides of this seal are found on the $1 bill; the side that bears the eagle is also referred to as "the Seal of the President of the United States." This seal contains several sets of the number 13:

1. The eagle holds 13 arrows and an olive branch with 13 olives and 13 leaves.

2. There is a cluster of stars over the eagle made up of 13 stars (representing the original 13 colonies).

3. The motto held in the eagle's beak, E Pluribus Unum (Out of Many, One) contains 13 letters.

4. There are 39 letters on the pyramid side of the shield. 39= 3x13

5. And perhaps most notably, the pyramid has 12 courses, capped by the 13th level: the all-seeing eye of God.

While it is not essential to the process of ascension for you to understand the mathematic/geometric concepts contained in this book, those of you who enjoy this type of material will get plenty of food for thought in this section. When regarding this material I ask you to notice the numerological aspects of the numbers we find in this system, and that all of these numbers reduce to either 7 or 9. The number seven governs cycles in nature and the law of the octave. The number nine is the number of the "number of completion." (144,000 – 1+4+4=9)

The use of the number 144,000 as the "harmonic of light" comes to us through the research of Bruce Cathie. Mr. Cathie, a former airline pilot and navigator, is one of the modern pioneers of planetary grid research. His original investigations, which eventually led him into planetary grid research, began in 1952 when he started tracking reports of UFO sightings in his native land of New Zealand.

While I cannot say that I have complete understanding of Mr. Cathie's theories, it does appear that he has apparently discovered some profound truths that can be used resolve to Einstein's Unified Field theory, and prove that, as Professor Einstein theorized, the unified field is governed (but not necessarily limited) by the speed of light.

Mr. Cathie's research offers evidence to suggest that the speed of light is directly related to rotation. This theory is supported by the assertion of renowned physicist, Arthur Young, that there are only two absolutes in the universe: rotation and the speed of light. The correlation between rotation and the speed of light is the key to moving between dimensions in the practice of the Merkaba meditation. The constant of 144,000 also suggests that the Mayan calendar has a relation to the speed of light and rotation, as the great cycle of the Mayan calendar of 5,200 – 360-day years is a period of 144,000 13-day cycles that equate to our weeks.

Bruce Cathie bases his theories on the rotational constant of the universe in relation to light. As Mr. Cathie points out, our lengths of measure (inch, foot, mile, meter, etc.) are arbitrary. No one knows what the "statute mile" might originally have been based on, but we do know that the metric system began during the French Revolution. In fact, the meter was originally based on the estimated diameter of our planet. In light of this it seems to make perfect sense for us to adopt a system of measurement for working with universal harmonics that is based directly on the speed of light and its relation to the circle.

To convert our standard time and distance measurements to light harmonics Mr. Cathie has developed a system that divides the Earth into 27 time zones, instead of the 24 we commonly use.* This allows us to base our time calculations on harmonics of the number 9 (2+7=9; 144,000/9=16,000; 1+6=7). By dividing the Earth into 27 zones instead of the usual 24 and then equating each of these zones to an hour containing 60 seconds, we end up with 97,200 seconds in a day (versus the 86,400 seconds in a regular day). This gives us a time differential of 9:8.

* Twenty seven is also a significant number in relation to the study of our planet's orbital mechanics, as the Moon takes 27 days to orbit the Earth, becoming full at 29.5 days, and averaging 28.

An important factor in considering these concepts is that while we consider the speed of light to be somewhat of an absolute, we still base our time measurements on the rotation of our planet. Because of this Mr. Cathie uses the 9:8 time differential to adjust the speed-of-light constant to Earth time and distances. This results in a reduction of the constant to figures of around 143,500 to 143,890 miles per "grid second," depending on how one manipulates the figures.

Those who are familiar with Mr. Cathie's work or who purchase his books and research them will find that I have skipped over a few details in order to make these concepts easier to convey in the limited space available here.

Ultimately, I suspect we will find that the spacefaring civilizations use a system of universal harmonic measurement that is based solely on degrees of arc, and that the universal standard for the speed of light will be 144,000 degrees of arc based on a circle that is approximately 25,000 statute miles in diameter (which by chance is roughly the diameter of our planet). In this system of measurement each degree of arc will equal a unit that is the philosophical equivalent of a mile, which in turn can be divided into smaller units of measure.

The mandala above was drawn by the author in 1988, shortly before he began his first book *Sedona Power Spot, Vortex, and Medicine Wheel Guide*. This mandala is based on the angle of the Great Pyramid.

DIVIDING THE ARC OF LIGHT

The arc, or *segment of a circle*, has been used since ancient Egypt to signify light and the God-quality that produces light. The symbol that was employed by the Egyptians is referred to as the Arc of Ray (which is an arc inscribed over a vesica piscis, or "God's eye," in a pentagram). In this instance we must understand that the term *"ray"* is synonymous with *Ra*, the solar deity of the Egyptians.

Ra is light. It is from this name that we get the words ray, rainbow, radiation and so on. According to the principles of sacred geometry, each level or octave in the electromagnetic spectrum (from sound to cosmic rays) is divided into seven sublevels. When we divide a circle of 360 degrees into seven segments and then draw rays (a proper geometrical term) from the segments at the edge of the circle to the center, we find that the inner angle (vertex) is very close to the angle of the Great Pyramid. One of the theories as to why the Great Pyramid does not employ this exact angle is that small variations are necessary for the proper movement of energy within the time field. If everything were exact, there would be no movement in time – our universe would crystalize.

Another way of looking at this is to relate these concepts to our knowledge of electronics. When radio operators tune up their transmitters, they find a setting on the controls where the system reaches its highest state of resonance; then they de-tune the system slightly. This is done because when the system is in perfect resonance the energy does not move through the antenna properly.

In relation to this I refer the reader to Andrija Puharich's book on Uri Geller, *Uri*. In this book Dr. Puharich relates their encounters with a group of extraterrestrial intelligences who refer to themselves as "The Nine" (the Nine Principles of Existence – sound familiar?). In this book the Nine encourage humanity to look within for the answers to our problems: The Nine assure us that each human has the ability to perform acts of ESP, to move objects with thought, and to physically transport the body with thought! The key to this, they say, is to be able to **increase the electrical energy within the body seven times** "normal." (See *Uri*, page 252.)

According to the Nine, when this occurs our "corresponding approximation to light velocity" will be 99%, and at this point we will achieve "infinitization" (ascension?). Looking at the numerology of this we find that the number 7 is the final result (99% = 9+9=18; 1+8=9; 144000/9=16,000; 1+6=7).

NUMEROLOGY

It is important to be aware of the numerological significance and the relationships of the numbers. If you are not familiar with this concept, I will give you a brief overview: There are only nine numbers in our mathematic system. Each of these numbers represents a universal quality. The number ten is unity; it is the synthesis of 0 (the void) and 1 (the first cause). The number ten represents that which we call God, which is in turn the synthesis of the other nine universal qualities. In numerology, when considering the significance of numbers higher than 9, all the numbers in the figure are added together to arrive at a single number (144,000 = 1+4+4=9).

A NOTE ON THE NATURE OF LIGHT

In spiritual and metaphysical thought it is commonly believed that there are two distinct forms of light: physical light and spiritual Light (capital "L"). This essay deals with physical light. In our universe, the physical light that we see with our eyes is produced by stars. (All artificial light from lightbulbs, candles, etc., is star energy that has been captured and recycled in some way.) Starlight is the product of hydrogen fusion. Hydrogen is apparently the most abundant element in our universe.

The heavens are populated by a great number of stars, which continuously emit light in all directions, totally illuminating all interstellar space we can conceive of. When we gaze out into the heavens at night and see darkness between the stars, it is only because the majority of photons emitted from these stars travel off in directions that do not converge with our eyes. In other words, the darkness of space is only an illusion. Interstellar space is completely illuminated at all times; in fact, the universe is a **sea of light.**

It is interesting to note that we associate the word ray (light) with water (as in "rain" and "rainbow"). Could this have anything to do with the fact that the elements that form water, hydrogen and oxygen, are also two of the most abundant elements in stars? (Particularly hydrogen, but there are significant amounts of oxygen produced in the exterior of stars as well.) A poet might say that the stars *rain* light into the infinite sea of space.

As previously mentioned in the section of this book on sacred geometry, the underlying geometry of the planetary grid is the icosahedron. The icosahedron is composed of 12 pentagrams that interlock in a manner which is very similar to the interlocking circles of the Flower of Life. Each pentagram consists of five *arcs* of **72 degrees**, and five *rays* of **72 degrees** (72 is half of 144, which is a fractal of the light harmonic).

Taking into account what we now know about light harmonics and the elements of water and space, is it any surprise that our island of life in the great sea of space is based on the icosahedron?

Referring once again to the element hydrogen we must understand that it is the source of all physical light in the universe. In relation to this we should also understand that the primary element that makes up our physical body is hydrogen (not carbon) with oxygen coming in at a close second. Therefore, our bodies automatically have a high degree of resonance with stars! (and starlight...)

MERKABA

This Yantra is copied from a photograph taken by Drunvalo Melchizedek while visiting India. (Computer rendering by Michael Tyree.)

I feel that this Yantra, and the Yantra on the next page, the Sri Yantra, both have a direct relation to the Merkaba. I suggest that you photocopy both of these Yantras and use them for open-eye meditation targets. By breathing these energy diagrams into our minds we activate aspects of our consciousness that allow us to achieve increasingly higher attunements with Universal Life-Force Energies.

The drawing of the Sri Yantra above was made by Patrick Flanagan using a wire frame drawing program that allows lines to be drawn with an accuracy of eight decimal places.

I met the Flanagans while shopping for groceries. Our common interest in the Sri Yantra and metaphysics resulted in them writing the following chapters. For more information about their research, contact them through the address given at the end of the chapter.

Patrick and Gael Flanagan are well-known authors and professional health and longevity researchers whom you may be aware of already. Patrick is perhaps best known as the author of the 1970's best seller: *Pyramid Power*. Gael and Patrick are the first couple in recorded history to have been married in the Great Pyramid. Before meeting Patrick, Gael Crystal Flanagan had already established her career as a nationally known lecturer, writer, researcher, and nutritional consultant who was deeply involved in metaphysics, healing, and crystals. Together, they represent one of the most knowledgeable and talented research teams in the fields of life extension and metaphysics. They both hold doctoral degrees in alternative medicine, and their water-related research was nominated for a Nobel prize in 1994.

Patrick was one of the "boy geniuses" you may have heard about during the 50's and 60's. When he was 11 years of age he sold his first patented electronic device to the United States Air Force. After this he went on to invent his famous *Neurophone*, a device that is capable of sending electromagnetic sound frequencies directly into the brain. Largely because of this he was invited to do research at the "prestigious" Huyck research group in 1963.

It was while at the Huyck institute that Patrick met Dr. Henry Coanda. During his career Dr. Coanda made important basic discoveries about the science of fluid dynamics that have far-reaching applications. It is interesting to note that Dr. Coanda's research defined the ability of aircraft wings to develop enough lift to carry aircraft aloft. This important field of research also led to a great deal of research into the nature of Vortex energy in fluid dynamics. The science of fluid dynamics is one of the most important realms of physics, as large magnetic fields obey some of the laws of fluid dynamics. Check your dictionary for "Magnetohydrodynamic."

Dr. Coanda was very interested in water, not only as a hydrodynamic substance, but also as a life-giving substance. In the following chapter this will be discussed in more detail.

PRANA: LIFE-FORCE ENERGY
by Patrick Flanagan & Gael Crystal Flanagan

After reading a few hundred books on esoteric subjects I found that there were over 700 words for the Universal Life-Force Energy we call Prana. For example, the Chinese call this energy Chi, the Koreans call it Ki, the Tibetans call it Tumo. Prana is said to be the intrinsic energy that gives us life. In Sanskrit, the word Prana means "absolute energy." Because of the lack of consensus on terminology I decided to create a modern term to describe the Universal Life-Force energies that I work with and study. After giving this idea a great deal of thought I came up with the word "Innergy®." I have registered this word as one of my trademarks because I am a professional health researcher and inventor, and it is important that I have terms like this that distinguish my work and my products.

As long as we have abundant Prana we remain healthy and vital. If our reserve of Prana becomes low we lose our vitality and risk becoming sickly. Prana is circulated through the body and used as an energy source in much the same manner as the oxygen we breathe. Prana is essential to the functioning of the central nervous system and is used as a type of fuel – Innergy®. Every thought, every act, every effort of the *Will*, every motion of a muscle, uses up a certain amount of Prana. So if we want to remain healthy we should do things that maintain high levels of Prana in our body.

I have developed electronic devices that can measure the amount of Prana in the human body. Using these devices I have been able to identify various things that have an effect on the level of Prana in the body. It will probably not surprise you to find that common breath exercises, as taught in the schools of yoga, have the ability to increase the Prana charge of the human body, and that exercise also plays a role in either replenishing Prana or dissipating Prana. Sleep also plays an important part in energizing and repolarizing our bio-energy fields.

My research has also determined that the water we drink has profound effects on the level of Innergy® in the body. This is because water is one of the primary vehicles of life-force energy. Good drinking water, and lots of it, is more important than many people realize, not only because water flushes out toxins but because water has the ability to energize, or de-energize the body. Pure, low-mineral water is essential to a high level of health as the body needs the purest water possible in order to synthesize the special water that exists within the cells. This water is in the form of a liquid crystal and it has the ability to transmit light between cells.

Crystals naturally resonate with life-force energy because they are highly structured. One of the wonders of water is that the more structured it is, the more life-force energy it will contain. *You will probably find it interesting to note that one of the most desirable forms of liquid crystal water is composed of groups of water molecules that are organized into star tetrahedrons.*

I have been studying the mystery of life from a scientific perspective for years, and I have found that while life-force energy has components that defy accepted scientific analysis, there are also aspects of this energy that do correspond to known physical phenomena such as light and electrical/magnetic energy. As an example of this I will note that scientists in China have discovered a physical basis for the energy pathways we call acupuncture meridians.

These scientists have discovered that the acupuncture meridians resemble fiber optic channels similar to those used in telecommunications. These *tubules* are about a hundred microns in diameter. They act like dielectric wave-guides that carry energy through the body and control the functions of the organs. *What this implies is that the energy that travels through these channels is a form of light.*

I also find it interesting to note that Dr. Harold Saxon Burr, a professor from Yale University, has discovered that every living organism is controlled by an electrical energy-field structure. He has named these electrical fields L-Fields or life-fields. His book, *Blueprint for Immortality* summarizes the discoveries he made during his 40 years of research.

One of Dr. Burr's most thought provoking discoveries has been that eggs and seeds are surrounded by electrical fields that resemble the organism they are designed to reproduce. As an example, chicken eggs are surrounded by electrical fields that have the shape of a chicken, and flower seeds are girdled by electrical fields that have the shape of a flower. If these electrical fields are absent, the seed or the egg will not produce, it is already dead, whether it appears to be dead or not: it has lost its vitality.

On the human body the life-fields can be detected and measured with silver chloride electrodes and a sensitive instrument known as an electrometer. The primary energy paths follow the same pattern as acupuncture meridians mapped by the Chinese thousands of years ago! These fields are a measure of a person's vitality: if the field is strong, the body is strong, if the field is weak, the body is weak.

Using his sensitive equipment, Dr. Burr has been able to detect cervical cancer months or years before it became a physical reality. He said that all disease is first manifested as a change in the body's electrical blueprint before it becomes a physical reality. This is why bad habits eventually manifest as physical disease. People often weaken their bio-fields daily for years before they become sick. In contrast, if we re-balance our bio-energy fields on a daily basis we can prevent illness from manifesting. Disease doesn't come on suddenly, it first develops in our bio-energy fields.

The research of Dr. Burr and the scientists in China seems to indicate that life-force energy exists as both an electrical field and as a type of energy that is similar to light. What this also implies is that these energies are an aspect of another force that is much more subtle and difficult to detect, but quite possibly more powerful.

The Sanskrit word Yantra means "geometric power diagram".

The Sri Yantra (Sri means high, great, or exalted) is said to be the most powerful of all known geometric power symbols. I have been interested in the Sri Yantra for years, and I have found that this symbol is more than just a pretty design, it is a light-wave antenna that has the ability to focus life-force energy, balance life-force energy, and increase the level of life-force energy.

It is said that meditation on the Sri Yantra will bring enlightenment and that all the secrets of the universe will be revealed to the person who mediates on it until its image is engraved in the mind. We know a very famous and successful Hollywood producer who had a special room in his mansion where he had a huge Sri Yantra painted on one of the walls. The only furniture in this room was a hydraulic chair that was designed to lift him into the air in front of the Sri Yantra. He meditated on it every day, and believed that this Yantra gave him the power to succeed.

All true Yantras consist of geometric designs that are framed by a square that has four "gates" that respect the powers of the four directions. In this frame are two circles of lotus blossoms that have the specific number of petals each particular Yantra requires. These lotus rings enclose a set of concentric circles that border the geometric power diagram. Philosophically we can see a definite parallel between a living lotus flower, which is a light-receptor, and the lotus petals of the Yantra, which appear to perform a function that is similar to that of an antenna dish that directs energy to the antenna array in its center.

Some books on Yantras say that the secret to drawing a perfect Sri Yantra is only given to a chosen few in a secret monastery in Tibet. Over the years I have seen many Sri Yantra representations, but none were perfect. The geometry of the Sri Yantra is very advanced, and while it might appear that any good draftsman could produce a Sri Yantra easily, they would soon discover themselves lost. Since I originally became aware of this design and the powers associated with it, I have attempted to draw it, and have now spent 25 years perfecting it.

The Sri Yantra is deceptively simple. It looks like it would be easy to draw, but there are so many variables it is almost impossible to make all the triangles fit together in a way that is completely harmonious or that reflects a design constant throughout. There are no books available that show how to draw this design correctly, and I never saw a perfect Sri Yantra until I penetrated its mystery.

My early drawings 25 years ago looked fairly good, as the lines were thick enough to cover up imperfections. With the development of the personal computer, however, I became frustrated because the drawing programs are accurate to a millionth of an inch. This means that slight irregularities become painfully obvious. Ultimately, I spent hundreds of hours trying to draw the Sri Yantra on the computer – without success.

I finally reached a point where I felt that I had spent enough time on this project that I must certainly have become eligible to have the secret revealed to me. I therefore resolved to mentally ask our spiritual teacher Sri Sathya Sai Baba of

India to help me. That evening he appeared in my dreams and showed me the secrets of the Sri Yantra. The next morning I drew one to an accuracy of one 10,000,000th of an inch!

The center of a perfect Sri Yantra is made up of 27 straight lines. These lines form five triangles that point down and four triangles that point up. These triangles are interlaced so that line intersections are at perfect points. This means that the geometry of each triangle must exactly complement that of all the other triangles. In the exact center of the Yantra is a tiny dot or point that is known as the "bindu" or creation point. When the Yantra is used as a focus for meditation, the observer stares at the bindu point.

The Sri Yantra is said to represent the geometric structure of the sound of creation – OM. The Hindu story of creation says that God spoke one word (OM) and the universe was created. It is said that the experienced meditator will hear the sound of creation or the universal OM once he transcendentally enters the field of creation. This is similar to the Christian story of creation. "In the beginning was the Word..." The Christian story does not, however, give the word. Was it OM?

One of the most interesting things that should be noted about OM and the Sri Yantra is that the work of Dr. Hans Jenny has demonstrated that they have a scientifically demonstrable energetic connection that is not only quite amazing, it also demonstrates the significance of metaphysics as a science.

Dr. Hans Jenny is the developer of a field of scientific research know as Cymatics (the C is pronounced like a K). One of his primary research devices consists of a horizontal metal plate that is connected to a device that is very similar to the driver coil in a typical loudspeaker. This device is able to send sound vibrations directly into the metal plate. During his experiments Dr. Jenny would cover the plate with sand or liquid and observe the wave patterns that the sound vibrations produced in the material on the plate.

Dr. Jenny discovered that various musical tones and other types of sounds produce distinct standing wave patterns as geometric forms in the sand. These patterns could then be photographed or filmed with a video camera, and he has published a series of books containing hundreds of these vibration pictures which he refers to as 'kinematic' patterns.

What we find particularly interesting about this is that when Dr. Jenny chanted the word OM into his apparatus, a perfect Sri Yantra pattern was formed in the vibrating sand! This discovery appears to prove the ancient Hindu assertion that the Sri Yantra represents the sound of OM.

In 1972, after 20 years of research I published my first book, *Pyramid Power*. This book was enormously popular and approximately 1.5 million copies were sold. In retrospect I find it interesting to note that this book created a noticeable shift in the consciousness of America, and that it became one of the catalysts for the current New Age movement.

Pyramid Power is about the mysteries of life-energy and life-energy's relation to phenomena associated with the Great Pyramid of Egypt. One of the most important things that can be said about the Great Pyramid geometries is that these angles create a resonant structure that either produces or focuses energies that are associated with life, and that these energies exist as very high frequency microwaves in the 10-micrometer band, which is close to the frequencies of visible light.

Shortly before I published Pyramid Power, Karel Drbal of Czechoslovakia patented a Styrofoam pyramid model and sold it as a "razor blade sharpener." His patent application stated that the device was a *cosmic* microwave resonator.

Karel had discovered that he could use the same razor for hundreds of shaves if he kept the blades inside his pyramid model. As a testimony to the effectiveness of this we can take note of the fact that he sold thousands of these devices in Europe, and that the patent examiner who granted this patent tried this pyramid and was able to shave 200 times with a blade that normally gave him only three or four shaves.

Karel's theory was that the pyramid focused *cosmic* (etheric?) microwaves into the steel of the razor blade, and that this energy kept the blade sharp by accelerating the spin of the water molecules that had become trapped in the crystal matrix of the blade, thus causing them to be expelled from the steel before it has a chance to rust. He also speculated that the energy from the pyramid had the ability to repair the crystalline structure of the blade.

It should be noted that in 1969 the United States Atomic Energy Commission, the Smithsonian Institution, and Ein Shams University in Cairo combined their efforts in an attempt to use natural cosmic rays from deep space to X-ray the Great Pyramid, in the hope that they might find hidden chambers. As you may be aware, certain types of cosmic rays penetrate physical matter. Because of this the scientists in charge of this project hoped they could use their sensitive equipment to locate places where there were variations in the amounts of cosmic rays detected, thus revealing hidden chamber. What the scientists found, however, is that from day to day their readings varied in an erratic manner that defied all known laws of physics. The project was ultimately abandoned, and one of the chief scientists made a public statement about strange occult forces.

In 1983 Gael and I became the first people in recorded history to have been married in the Great Pyramid at Giza.

In 1976 I met Dr. Phil Calahan, a professor at the University of Florida. Dr. Calahan was an energy expert who had discovered that insects communicate with infra red laser light. He had postulated that the inner energy control mechanisms of all living systems may be controlled and enhanced by coherent light that is identical to the light produced by some types of lasers.

In support of this theory, scientists who study "Information Theory" understand that cell division requires a significantly higher *signal to noise ratio* than that which can be supplied by the chemical interactions of DNA alone, and that ordinary electo-chemical nerve impulses cannot possibly account for the vast amount of data that is transferred between cells, or the speed at which some impulses travel in the human body. (The movements of virtuoso musicians often appear to exceed the speed limit of the central nervous system.)

Dr. Calahan developed a Fourier Transform Infrared Spectrometer that is able to detect coherent light signals from biological sources. I visited Dr. Calahan's laboratory and have had the opportunity to work with this device. When we tested the pyramid and Sensor® with his equipment we found that these devices continuously emit an energy that is apparently very similar to the coherent light energies that Dr. Calahan's equipment was tuned to detect. What this means to Gael and I is that the pyramid and the Sensor® are natural laser or maser amplifiers that use the primal technology of the universe to produce Prana – and that Prana must be very similar, energetically, to visible light.

This similarity between visible light and Pranic Life-Force Energy appears to demonstrate the physical universe has a phase of energy that cannot be directly detected by standard laboratory equipment. And that one aspect of this energy phase has a direct relation to physical light, yet it will remain forever hidden to our eyes. One might ask themselves, however: "Why is it that the pineal gland in the center of the brain contains cells that are almost identical to the light receptor cells in the eyes?"

Of special interest is the fact that Dr. Calahan discovered that the word OM also produced this same variety of coherent light energy in the human breath! When he chanted the word OM into the laser-light detection pathway of the spectrometer, it produced powerful coherent laser energy. This energy was produced only from the OM; no other sounds have been known to produce the same effect.

Dr. Calahan theorized that the coherent light energy produced by the breath is the result of organic molecules in the breath being excited by the sound vibration of Om. These excited molecules then emit invisible infra-red coherent light that is indistinguishable from light that is emitted by some types of laser beam machines. Dr. Calahan also theorizes that these laser signals are detected by special sensors in the skin of the meditator, and that in resonance to these light signals the brain alters its own chemistry and that of the body by releasing endorphins and other brain chemicals. This may be one of the reasons why people go into altered states when they chant mantras correctly. It is also interesting to note that these coherent light signals may well have the ability to affect other people. Perhaps this is why many people feel that chanting with other people has the ability to increase the power of the experience.

When compared side by side, our special Sensor® III pendant produced the same laser signals as the OM chant! Dr. Calahan said that the Sensor was an OM generator!

146

There are five places on earth where people often live to be more than 100 years of age while maintaining remarkably good health. These include Hunza land in northern Pakistan and the Vilcabamba in Ecuador. These people attribute their long lives to the type of water they drink. In all cases their water comes from blue ice glaciers that are millions of years old. Dr. Henri Coanda devoted his life to unlocking the secret of these special waters. Hunza type water is very much like distilled water in chemical analysis, but it has energy properties that are not found in distilled water. For example, fish die in distilled water but thrive in Hunza type water. The electrical properties of Hunza water were identified as anomalous physical properties not found in distilled water. Although he was able to identify the anomalous physical properties of Hunza type water, he failed in his attempts to re-create analogs of Hunza type water in his laboratory.

After we became good friends, Dr. Coanda turned his life-long water project over to me in 1963. By 1983, after 20 years of continued research, Gael Crystal and I discovered how to duplicate and concentrate these waters. Our discovery, which we trade-named "Crystal Energy®" concentrate," is the result of a 33-step manufacturing process. When Crystal Energy® is added to ordinary distilled water, it is transformed instantly into Hunza type water.

Assimilation of nutrients and vitamins from our foods is largely dependent on our body's ability to "wet" (dissolve) and process nutrients in the digestive system. Water's ability to wet foods depends on its "Zeta potential," (electrical charge) which, in turn, directly affects the surface tension of our digestive fluids.

Our work with water indicates that the level of health in the body is directly related to the structure of the water within individual cells. If the water in the cells is maintained at a high state of purity, and has a high Zeta potential, the vitality of the body will remain high. If the water in the cells becomes highly mineralized or polluted with other toxins, its electrical charge is then neutralized, thus compromising the structuring of the water and reducing the vitality of the body.

It is unfortunate that more people do not understand the importance of having the right kind of water in the diet. It is not only important to drink lots of water in order to rid the body of toxins, it is also very important to drink water that is high in Zeta potential. If water has a weak Zeta potential and contains excess minerals, individual cells cannot properly discharge their toxins. Ultimately this can lead to a general deterioration of health and loss of vitality. In fact, most people who are old and stiff are highly calcified on the cellular level.

WHAT MAKES IT WORK?

We discovered that the anomalous electrical properties discovered by Dr. Coanda were the result of a special type of colloidal mineral found in Hunza water. These minerals impart an electrical charge to water that is known as zeta potential. It was the study of these special colloidal minerals and ions that led to the development of our Crystal Energy® concentrate, which contains our special colloidal minerals: Flanagan Microcluster® colloids.The Flanagan Microcluster® minerals, which are found in Crystal Energy®, alter the structure of drinking water by acting like tiny electrical seed crystals that attract water molecules and form a liquid crystal lattice. This increases a measure known as free energy and also reduces the surface tension.

Microcluster® minerals are unique in that they have a very high electrical charge (Zeta potential) and are small enough to be easily utilized. The charge on ordinary colloidal minerals is not very high or very stable, so ordinary low energy colloidal minerals have little or no effect on the structure of water. Colloids that are found in dead sea beds and mineral clays are devoid of zeta potential and are too large to be used by the living system. Zeta potential represents a basic Law of Nature. It plays a vital role in all forms of plant and animal life. It is the force that maintains the discreteness of the billions of circulating cells that nourish the organism. Microcluster® minerals consist of elements and combinations of elements which are by definition in the smallest possible size range while still remaining molecules.

When Flanagan Microclusters® are diluted for drinking, they have such powerful surface energies that the resulting drop in surface tension is remarkable. In distilled water, the immediate drop is between 55 to 65 dynes per centimeter. If left for a period of time, the surface tension can gradually drop to a level as low as 33 dynes. Hunza water has a surface tension of 68, this means that water treated with Crystal Energy® concentrate has an even lower surface tension and a greater Zeta Potential.

FLANAGAN MICROCLUSTERS® CREATE LIQUID CRYSTAL STRUCTURES IN WATER

When water is structured with CRYSTAL ENERGY® the water molecules form a matrix based on the Dodecahedron. This liquid crystal matrix has the unique ability to capture and hold negatively charged Hydrogen Ions, that can deliver significant amounts of electrical energy to the body. **(See page 151 for more details.)**

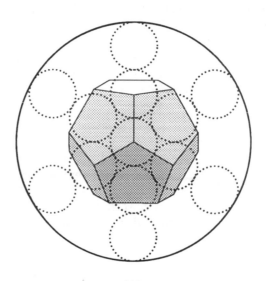

One of the key elements of this discussion is the understanding that organized structure is essential to the generation and transmission of subtle energies. Crystals are an excellent example of this: Because they have a uniform structure that acts as a natural low-distortion wave guide for many types of energy.

Magnets made from iron are another important example of how structuring produces wave guides for energy: a piece of iron becomes magnetic when the electrons in the iron atoms become uniformly polarized. (That is to say, when the electrons "line up," a magnetic field is produced.) This magnetic field appears to be a secondary effect of another energy that exists in a parallel phase with physical reality. Most establishment scientists are, however, loath to admit that this could be a possibility.

Structure is one of the keys to understanding the power of the great pyramid geometries. These angles act as waveguides for specific types of life-force energy that are also associated with the sound Om and the Sri Yantra.

The study of sacred geometry reveals the primal structure of the universe and demonstrates how physical matter is formed by light. I find it quite interesting that Drunvalo Melchizedek has suggested that if individual humans learn how to incorporate the knowledge of sacred geometry into their spiritual work they will receive the ability to tap into powerful forces.

Yantras are energy structuring devices that resonate with specific energies. In India and Tibet there are dozens of Yantras that are said to have various types of power. Like crystals, Yantras can be worn as jewelry that has the ability to increase the energy level of humans. One of the most powerful bio-energizers is the Sri Yantra.

I found early on that the Sri Yantra has a profound effect on the L-Field. Later, I combined this with specific geometric structures to produce devices that balance and energize the human bio-energy system. One of the results of this is my invention, the Sensor®. This device is technically a log periodic broad-band slot microwave antenna.

By 1974 I was producing and selling a number of devices that employ the power of geometrical structuring to either create or focus energies that balance and enhance bio-energy in the human body. I had tested and validated these devices with the Burr electrometer and with acupuncture energy instruments. These bio-energy devices included the flat pyramid design which we called the Sensor®. When this 'flat pyramid' is worn on the body it has a profound balancing effect on the acupuncture system. The Sensor® III is a geometric log periodic antenna design that has one of my earlier Sri Yantra designs in the center. (See illustration.)

In 1974 we were featured on the Tom Snyder Show on NBC. On this show, I used an esoteric martial arts technique to weaken Tom Snyder without him realizing what I was doing. I waved my hands in front of him and *without touching his body*, disturbed his energy field. A moment later he said that he that felt like he was going to fall down because he felt extremely weak. I then rejuvenated him by letting him hold one of my Sensors®. Without any coaching on my part Tom said that he felt stronger when he touched the Sensor®.

Sensor® III design was made into a piece of Innergy® jewelry. Several hundred thousand of these units were sold in the 1970's. The diamond shaped slots form a log-periodic spiral. One of my earlier Sri Yantra design is prominent in the center. I will suggest that although this is merely an ink design on paper, it is nonetheless sending subtle energy toward you as you gaze at it. (Copyright Patrick Flanagan)

LIGHT BODY ACTIVATION AND LIFE EXTENSION
WITH FLANAGAN TECHNOLOGY — THE FUEL OF THE STARS

Due to the numerous requests for information on how to obtain Patrick and Gael Flanagan's CRYSTAL ENERGY® water treatment drops, I have included **ordering information** (see next page). Their latest invention, **MICROHYDRIN**™ was released in October of 1997, I feel that there is an excellent possibility that this product will be found to increase the body's natural ability to work with Life Force Energy and Light, and that it may be one of the keys to the realization of the dream of the New Age: **to become a being who lives on Light**. It is the fuel of the stars.

ONE OF THE MOST IMPORTANT BIOLOGICAL DISCOVERIES OF ALL TIME

MICROHYDRIN™ is the invention of the renowned scientists, Patrick and Gael Flanagan. I feel that independent peer review of this invention and its related systems in the human body will result in this invention being universally recognized as one of the most important biological discoveries of all time, and that everyone who wants to improve their life and live a longer, healthier life will ultimately want to use MICROHYDRIN™ **it is that good**.

MICROHYDRIN™contains potent hydrogen ions that carry loosely bound electrons. Because hydrogen is so small, each capsule contains as many biologically available electrons as approximately 10,000 glasses of orange juice. Yet it is completely non-toxic, and safe at normal dosages.

Electrical activity in the body is everything. More than anything else, our bodies need the energy of the free electrons that we get from the food, water and air we consume. These electrons are the life-force that "burns" oxygen within every cell. The level of vitality in the body, and its resistance to disease and aging has a direct reaction to the average level of free electrons that are available in the body.

The body behaves like a common battery in that it can be charged with electrons, and also depleted of electrons. Most diseases, from the common cold to cancer, can only exist in a body that has a low charge. Unfortunately, most common drinking water (including purified water), processed foods, and polluted air, contain far too little free electrons to maintain desirable electrical levels in the body.

On the cellular level, aging in the body is caused by oxidation. This process is the result of oxygen atoms taking electrons from the various molecules that make up our cells. This oxidation of the molecules results in what is known as "free radical production." Antioxidants such as vitamin C, vitamin E, beta carotene, etc. have only one function in the fight against oxidation in the body - they deliver electrons to oxidized free-radical molecules within the body.

In the neutralization of free-radicals each vitamin molecule has only one electron to give, after that the vitamin itself becomes a free-radical that must in turn be neutralized by another vitamin. This phenomenon is known as "electron cascade." The hydrogen ions contained in MICROHYDRIN™ are the most powerful and universally effective antioxidant and **anti aging** nutrients known, and they are capable of reacting with any type of free radical, at any point in the electron cascade. This is a very important point to remember.

MICROHYDRIN™ has an average of 18x10 to the 23rd power electrons in an average capsule. This amazing number of electrons is made possible both by the minute size of hydrogen and the advanced delivery system of tiny microcrystals that protect the electrical charge of the hydrogen.

WATER is made from the elements we burn in our cells to produce life; **hydrogen and oxygen**. In metaphysics it is said that the power of Love holds hydrogen and oxygen together. The light and life that is created when this chemical bond is made is the same power that propelled the Saturn Five boosters that sent Apollo to the moon. For the first time, we are able to put the refined essience of this force into our bodies, let us imagine what this will do for our Light Bodies?

LIVE LONGER, LIVE BETTER, EAT LIGHT!

Please note that the original intention for the inclusion of material on Patrick and Gael Flanaga's' work was not to promote or sell their products. The inclusion of advertising in this edition is due to the fact that the material that originally appeared in these final pages of the first three editions of this book was no longer relevant. The Flanagans' inventions that are mentioned here have great potential, and I feel that making them available to the readers of this book is in perfect harmony with our goal of raising the vibration of the planet.